THE OSGOOD FILES

ALSO BY CHARLES OSGOOD

Nothing Could Be Finer Than a Crisis That Is Minor in the Morning

There's Nothing I Wouldn't Do If You Would Be My POSSLQ

*Osgood on Speaking: How to Think on Your Feet
Without Falling on Your Face*

THE
OSGOOD
FILES

Charles Osgood

G. P. PUTNAM'S SONS
New York

G. P. Putnam's Sons
Publishers Since 1838
200 Madison Avenue
New York, NY 10016

Library of Congress Cataloging-in-Publication Data
Osgood, Charles.
The Osgood files / Charles Osgood.
p.   cm.
I. Title.
PN4874.O78A25   1991   90-44048 CIP
814'.54—dc20
ISBN 0-399-13569-3

Printed in the United States of America
3   4   5   6   7   8   9   10

This book is printed on acid-free paper.
∞

ACKNOWLEDGMENTS

With heartfelt thanks to my CBS Radio News colleagues Phil Chin, Harry Polosjian, and Ed Sentner, who somehow put "The Osgood File" on radio four times each morning; to Jim Ganser, who produces the television version on CBS *This Morning;* to Randy Joyce, Alan Golds, and Dick Jefferson, who whisper into my ear through my little anchorman's earpiece; to my assistant Lori Knight, without whom I wouldn't know what to do next; to Maureen Schoos and Gail Lee, who've come up with so many good ideas; to Mike Argirion, Stacy Deibler, and Evelyn Smith of Tribune Media Services, who made an old broadcast guy's prose come out looking like newspaper columns; to Ralph Mann and Esther Newberg of ICM for solving so many problems. And special appreciation to Neil Nyren, who thought there might be a book in there somewhere, and whose support and encouragement saw it through.

For my wife, Jean, and our five children:
Kathleen, Winston, Anne Elizabeth, Emily Jean, and Jamie,
without whom this book would not have been necessary.

Contents

III. CURRENT AFFAIRS

IV. THE PURSUIT OF HAPPINESS

V. THIS OLD HOUSE

VI. SEASONS

THE OSGOOD FILES

Preface

Writing for print is quite different from writing for radio or television. In broadcasting, the words disappear literally at the speed of light. A given statement has the potential to make you look foolish only for a moment. If you are on a network broadcast, what you say has to hold true for all of three hours until the last West Coast feed. Typically, the thought travels into a microphone, from the mike to the transmitter, and then out into the world at large, where it passes with equal swiftness in one ear, out the other, and on into space. Theoretically, the signal keeps going on and on at 186 thousand miles per second to the edge of the solar system, and then on into outer space to the outer reaches of the universe. Fortunately, as far as we know, there are no receivers out there. At this very moment, one of my old broadcasts may be whizzing past Betelgeuse or Alpha Centauri. The facts may have changed completely, but who cares? Nobody up there is likely to complain. There's no calling the signal back and this is, in most cases, a blessing, believe me.

By contrast, the pieces in this book come mostly from newspaper columns; either the humor column I used to write for *USA Weekend*, or the twice-weekly syndicated newspaper pieces I do now for Tribune Media Services. These pieces are not exactly designed for permanence or engraved on stone, but since they can be held in the hand and even passed around, I can never be sure how long they will hang around to embarrass me. In these fast-moving times, it is difficult to say anything that will still be true three hours hence, not to mention three weeks or seven months later. The way to extend the embarrassment potential almost indefinitely is to collect the pieces and put them in a book. This is what we have done here.

Beyond that, there is a big difference between listening to something on a broadcast and reading it in print. If something doesn't make sense to you on the air, you just shrug and figure you must have missed something. But if something doesn't make sense in print, you can go back a few lines and try to pick up the thread. If it still doesn't make any sense the second or third time around, the reader has every reason to conclude that it never made any sense in the first place. What I'm saying is that you can get away with more in hot air than you can in cold print.

—CHARLES OSGOOD

I

NOTHING LIKE
RECOGNITION,
I ALWAYS SAY

Newspapers

Nobody takes you seriously in the journalism business, even the electronic end of the journalism business, unless you can prove that you have paid your journalistic dues as an "ink-stained wretch." In other words, in order to earn your stripes as a reporter, you're supposed to have worked for a newspaper.

It just so happens that, like H. L. Mencken, I grew up in Baltimore, Maryland, and at a tender age went to work for a newspaper. Like Mencken, I was associated with the *Sun* papers. Although I never wrote for a newspaper in my Baltimore days, I was definitely one of those "ink-stained wretches."

I was a paperboy. I'd get up early in the morning and go out to the street corner where the truck had left the papers all bound up with wire. I'd cut the wire, count the papers (always was a suspicious type), then I'd get down on my right knee and balance the newspapers on my left leg so I could get the strap around the whole pile. The strap was a loop. One end went around my right shoulder, the papers wound up under my left arm. This freed up the right arm for purposes to be explained. The papers weighed about a ton . . . sometimes more than a ton, depending on how much news or advertising there was on a given day. In the process, I would get newsprint all over my hands, my arms, my shirt, my pants. I was an ink-stained wretch if ever there was one.

Then I'd struggle to my feet and start walking the paper route. As I approached each house, I would reach under the strap and pull out one copy. Holding my thumbs just so, in about one second flat, I'd snap the newspaper smartly, fold one end into the other, and wind up with a neat package that had exactly the same aerodynamics as a Frisbee. And Frisbees hadn't even been invented yet. Then, a smooth backswing, a flip of the wrist, and the folded newspaper would sail majestically through the air, land gently on the front of the porch, and slide gracefully to a stop on the doormat. Sometimes.

In my reverie, looking back through the haze of these many decades, all the papers ended up right on the doormat, although in fact, I'll bet a certain percentage of the throws went off course and the newspapers ended up in the bushes or on the roof. Yes, it all comes back to me now. Some of them did end up in the bushes and on the roof. No question about it.

Come to think of it, I am still delivering the news early in the morning, and have trouble sometimes being on target. Things haven't changed *that* much in forty years. Sometimes, even to this day, my hands will reach for a newspaper, my thumbs will find the right spots and, snap, flip, tuck, there's the old fold.

"See that chair?" I said to a colleague this morning, pointing to a chair all the way down the hall. "Watch this." The gentle backswing, the flick of the wrist, and the paper went sailing, twisting gently with that familiar Frisbee spin on it, and came down in a three-point landing, precisely on the designated chair.

"I'm impressed," said the colleague. I smiled. Inside I was beaming. The old newsboy hasn't lost the touch.

Our Finest Hour

Only occasionally do most reporters or correspondents get to "anchor" a news broadcast. Anchoring, you understand, means sitting there in the studio and telling some stories into the camera and introducing the reports and pieces that other reporters do. It looks easy enough. It is easy enough, most of the time . . .

It was back when I was relatively new at CBS News. I'd been in the business a while, but only recently had moved over to CBS News. I was old, but I was new. It was a Saturday night and I was filling in for Roger Mudd on the *CBS Evening News*. Roger was on vacation. The regular executive producer of the broadcast, Paul Greenberg, was on vacation, too. And so was the regular cameraman and the regular editor and the regular director. Somewhere along the line we had one too many substitutes that night.

I said "Good evening" and introduced the first report and turned to the monitor to watch it. What I saw was myself looking at the monitor. Many seconds passed. Finally there was something on the screen. A reporter was beginning a story. It was not the story I had introduced. Instead, it was a different story by a different reporter. This was supposed to be the second item in the newscast. So I shuffled my script around and made the first piece second and the second piece first. When I came back on camera, I explained what it was we had seen and reintroduced the first piece. Again there was a long, awkward pause. I shuffled my papers. I scribbled on the script. I turned to the monitor. Finally, the floor director, who was filling in for the regular floor director, cued me to go on. So I introduced the next report. It didn't come up either, so I said we'd continue in just a moment. Obvious cue for a commercial, I thought, but it took a while to register in the control room. When a commercial did come up, there was a frantic scramble in the studio to reorganize what was left of the broadcast. But by now everything had come undone.

When the commercial was over, I introduced a piece from Washington. What came up was a series of pictures of people who seemed to be dead. One man was slumped over a car wheel. Two or three people were lying in the middle of the street. Another man was propped up against the wall of a building, his eyes staring vacantly into space. Then came the voice of Peter Kalisher. "This was the town where everyone died," he said. I knew nothing whatsoever about this piece. It was not scheduled for the broadcast. Peter Kalisher was in Paris as far as I knew. But there had been nothing on the news wires about everybody in Paris having died. In the "fishbowl," the glassed-in office where the executive producer sits, there were at least three people yelling into telephones. Nobody in there knew anything about this piece either. The story was about some little town in France that was demonstrating the evils of cigarette smoking. Seems the population of the town was the same number as smoking-related deaths in France in a given year. It was a nice story well told, but since nobody in authority at CBS News, New York, had seen it or knew what was coming next, they decided to dump out of it and come back to me. I, of course, was sitting there looking at the piece with bewilderment written all over my face, when suddenly, in the midst of all these French people pretending to be dead, I saw myself, bewilderment and all.

All in all, it was not the finest broadcast CBS News has ever done. But the worst part came when I introduced the "end piece," a feature story that Hughes Rudd had done about raft racing on the Chatahoochie River. Again, when I finished the introduction, I turned to the monitor and, again, nothing happened. Then, through the glass window of the "fishbowl," I heard a loud and plaintive wail. "What the **** is going on?" screamed the fill-in executive producer. I could hear him perfectly clearly, and so could half of America. The microphone on my tie-clip was open. Standing in the control room watching this, with what I'm sure must have been great interest, was a delegation of visiting journalists from the People's Republic of China. They must have had a really great impression of American electronic journalism. The next Monday morning, sitting back at the radio desk where I belonged, I became aware of a presence standing quietly next to my desk. It was Richard Salant, the wise and gentle man who was then president of CBS News. He'd been waiting until I finished typing a sentence before bending over and inquiring softly: "What the **** *was* going on?"

The Lecture Life

One Friday afternoon right after lunch, I got a phone call from Bob Keedick. The Keedick family has been in the lecture business for a long time. Bob's father used to book Lowell Thomas's famous talks on "Lawrence in Arabia" before there was such a thing as radio. Anyway, Bob had a problem. Rex Reed, the movie columnist, was supposed to be speaking at a dinner in Phoenix that very night and had come down with such a bad case of laryngitis he couldn't talk at all. Could I hop on the next flight to Phoenix and fill in? I'd been up since four o'clock in the morning New York time, but aside from that, I couldn't think of a good reason not to go and the price was right, so off I went.

It was the annual dinner of a Phoenix business group, and everybody seemed quite relieved when I showed up. However disappointed that Rex Reed couldn't make it they might have been, they showed me nothing but courtesy and hospitality. There was a little cocktail reception for the head-table guests before the dinner, and then we all filed into the main dining room. Turned out to be a big dinner, several hundred people, all the movers and shakers of the Phoenix business world, it seemed to me.

The president of the organization explained to me that most of the people in the room would have no way of knowing that Rex Reed hadn't made it. There was a very nice picture of Rex Reed on the banquet program. I could see people at the tables looking at the picture of Rex Reed on the program and then looking up at me. I could imagine what they were whispering to each other: "Reed doesn't look anything like his picture, does he?"

After a full meal, dessert, coffee, some announcements, introduction of officers, acknowledgment of committees, handing out of awards, acceptances, preliminary remarks, etc., it was my turn. The introduction was most gracious. Rex Reed had this terrible case of laryngitis, but they were most fortunate indeed that CBS News correspondent Charles Osgood could be there and so on.

I started out by apologizing that I was unable to talk about movie stars since I didn't know any movie stars. In fact, I admitted, I didn't even know Rex Reed. But I spoke about news broadcasting for twenty minutes or so, explaining the sort of assignments I'd been getting, talking about Walter Cronkite, Dan Rather, people like that. The audience was attentive. They laughed at the right places and frowned at the right places, and when I finished, they applauded as if they meant it. I was right pleased with myself. Then it was time for questions. The first question was this:

"Mr. Reed, why do they have to use all those dirty words in the movies these days?"

Disney World

Disney World in Florida is a great place, and most everybody who's been there has delightful memories of it. Personally, however, when I think of Disney World, I always think of vomit. That may strike you as a bit odd, but you would understand if you had been along when Jean and I took the kids there. There were three of them. Kathleen was five years old, Winston was three, and Annie was one. Some kind of bug got us, and one after another we all got sick and threw up. It was a veritable festival of vomit.

We went gamely on, however, nobody wanting to spoil the fun for the rest. One sunny afternoon we were waiting in line for the "Small World" boatride. Kathleen had vomited that morning but was feeling much better. Winston had vomited the night before and did not seem his usual spirited self. Jean and I hadn't vomited yet, but our turns would come. This time, though, it was Annie's.

There was happy music coming over the loudspeaker. "It's a small world after all. It's a small world after all. It's a small world after all. It's a small, small world." Annie's face turned green. Her eyes got very big. We could all see what was happening. I picked her up and tried to get her away from all the folks, small and otherwise, waiting in the line, while Jean and the others went ahead with the ride. I almost made it, too. But not quite.

Before we could get back out to where we'd parked her stroller, she let go. All over herself. All over me. All over our clothes, our shoes, our hair. I took a diaper from the stroller . . . tried to wipe Annie's face, but here it came again. Most people passing gave us wide berth, which was smart of them, I think. But just as I was up to my elbows in more vomit than I care to think about, a fellow with a big smile on his face comes up . . . sticks out his hand and says, "Hi. You're Charles Osgood, CBS News, aren't you?"

Nothing like recognition, I always say.

Parenthood—1986

I am often asked how it came to pass that a quiet, unassuming fellow such as myself got to be named a Father-of-the-Year by the committee that names fathers of the year. My theory is that the committee got word of the fact that I had solved the Great Pizza Dilemma.

One evening a few months ago, I had occasion to take all five kids out for pizza. Now kids have quite definite ideas about what is edible, also called yummy, and what's inedible, better known as yucky. "I want mushrooms on mine," said Kathleen. "Mushrooms are yummy."

"Mushrooms are yucky," countered Winston. "I'll take pepperoni."

I was about to make a Solomon-like decision: One pepperoni pizza, one mushroom pizza, when up piped Annie. "I can't eat pepperoni and I can't eat mushrooms," she said. "Mushrooms and pepperoni are *both* yucky. I want sausage! Sausage is yummy."

"Sausage is yucky," several voices shot back. Kathleen and Winston were joined by Emily in this appraisal. "Let me get this straight," I said. "Kathleen wants mushrooms and won't eat pepperoni or sausage. Winston wants pepperoni and won't eat sausage or mushroom. Annie wants sausage and won't eat mushroom or pepperoni, and Emily doesn't want sausage. What *do* you want, Emily?"

Several of the kids tried to prompt Emily, but she had ideas of her own. "I *do* want sausage," she explained. "But I want it *with* mushrooms *and* pepperoni."

"Yuckeeee," came the instant chorus.

The only kid not expressing himself in this matter was Jamie, who wasn't quite two years old and not yet able to talk. Or maybe it's just that he couldn't get a word in edgewise. "Jamie," I said, "whisper into Daddy's ear what kind of a pizza you want." Jamie grinned and whispered something into my ear that sounded like "Boortznyagepn."

"You got it!" I told him. "I'll take two large pizzas please, both with extra cheese."

This happens to be the way I like it, but Jamie took the rap. The other kids thought the pizza was okay. Not as yummy as it would have been with *their* favorite, but not as yucky as it would have been with somebody else's.

So this is how I got to be a Father-of-the-Year. Unfortunately, the scheme will not work for solving the Great Pizza Dilemma next time out. Jamie is starting to talk.

Parenthood—1987

We have five children. That does not seem like such a big family to me, but by today's statistical standards, it is. They range in age from twelve to three. Kathleen is twelve, Winston ten, Annie eight, Emily six, and Jamie three. It is a sobering subject for reflection that if they all go to college for four years, I will have twenty years of tuitions to pay.

Ah, but what a joy for now to hear "the patter of little feet" around the house, you say. This is not quite accurate. Little feet do not patter. They klunk, they clop, they scrape and bang. Running up the stairs, three, four, or five pairs of little feet sound like a herd of wild elephants, like thunder, like an earthquake maybe, but not like anything that patters.

The other sound people think you hear in a house full of kids is "the laughter of children at play." What you actually hear when children are at play is the sound of fighting. You hear the sound of yelling and screaming like a banshee. The laughter of children at play is not the light, lilting laughter you read about in books, but the fiendish, derisive, mocking laughter that goes with dialogue that runs something like this:

"Ha, ha, ha."

"What are *you* laughing at?"

"Nothing."

"Oh yeah?"

"Yeah!"

"Says who?"

"Says you."

"I did not!"

"You did so!"

"Well, it isn't fair."

The decibel level is rising as this scintillating conversation goes on, and you know for sure that any time now the dispute will be referred to you for adjudication. This is a mistake on their part, but they never seem to learn. Bill Cosby is right: Grown-ups don't care about fairness; what grown-ups care about is quiet.

Another misconception is the notion that when a big family gathers around the dinner table, it is like a Norman Rockwell painting, with Mom and Dad beaming proudly as their little darlings chow down.

What actually happens is that the first one at the table (Kathleen) finishes eating and asks to be excused before the last one (Annie) sits down.

Civilized table conversation is limited because nobody ever gets to finish a sentence. It's not just that the kids interrupt each other, they won't let you finish a sentence either.

Don't get me wrong. I think the children are wonderful and big families are swell. It's just that—

As Time Goes By

When you were a kid, time moved at a glacial pace. In September, when school started, the year stretched out in front of you as something interminable. In June, the glorious thing about summer vacation was that it would last practically forever. Some of June, all of July, all of August, and some of September. That used to be a long, long time. Remember?

The kids who were two years older than you were older by far. More mature, more experienced. Teachers and parents were people whose lives, for all practical purposes, were over. They were old. They knew nothing. And kids just two years younger than you were babies. Impossibly naive and childish. They, too, knew nothing. Remember?

The astronomers insist that nothing has speeded up. They say the earth is still spinning at the same rate—one revolution per day—orbiting the sun at the same rate—one circuit per year. The atomic clocks show no acceleration. And yet, I know for certain that the twenty years between 1936 and 1956 passed very slowly. I know because I was there.

It's not as though there was nothing going on, mind you. We had World War II and several other notable events, which took a full twenty years to unfold. But somehow, the two decades between 1970 and 1990, on the other hand, shot by in about twenty minutes! Time has definitely speeded up, no matter what the astronomers and atomic physicists and their instruments say. Admittedly, this is based on my personal experience and not on any empirical evidence, but a lot of my friends who are my age tell me they have noticed the very same thing.

Nowadays, a day goes by in about an hour. A month seems like a week. A year takes about a month, month and a half. It took me and my contemporaries forever to grow up. We wanted to grow up, but it happened far too slowly to suit us. My kids are growing up overnight. Maybe it has something to do with diet.

Fortunately for me, during this same time period, when time has been speeding up so much, another remarkable phenomenon has taken place. In the 1950s, when time was creeping along so slowly, people who were in their forties were really quite old and decrepit. I can remember this quite distinctly. Now that time has speeded up so much, however, people who are now in their forties and even in their fifties seem very youthful and energetic. Even those in their sixties and seventies are beginning to look good.

It is a great disappointment to me that my very own children, who seem otherwise observant, have failed to notice either the progressive speeding up of time or the increasing youthfulness of middle-aged people. I don't know what's the matter with them, but to them it still seems a long wait from Christmas to Easter. To them an old song is something by Billy Joel. Ancient history is the Vietnam War. For them, too, the year 2000 is in the far-off future—nine years away. I try to explain that nine years *used* to be a long time, but that it isn't so anymore. They don't listen. And when I say that George Bush sure is a good-looking fellow, they give me the strangest look!

Bow Ties

———————

Many of you have been kind enough to send me clippings from an issue of *Success* magazine in which a so-called "clothing expert" by the name of John Molloy suggests that men who wear bow ties are "distrusted by almost everyone." Mr. Molloy, the author of books for people who don't know how to dress themselves, goes on to recommend that "if you have a bow tie . . . you leave it at home." If, however, you feel you must don a bow tie, Molloy proposes that you get the right accessories to go with it . . . "a red nose and a beanie cap with a propellor."

Since credibility and being trusted are important in my line of work, I suppose there are certain options now as to what I, as a bow tie–wearing news correspondent, should do.

1. I could immediately burn all my bow ties and run right out to buy several of the "rep" or diagonally striped four-in-hand ties that Mr. Molloy recommends for people who want other people to trust them.

2. I could keep on wearing the bow ties, but run right out and buy the beanie with the propellor to wear along with them. I do not know where to purchase such a

beanie, but I am sure Mr. Molloy could be helpful in that regard.

3. I could do nothing, continuing to wear bow ties while talking about news events, and completely ignoring Mr. Molloy's valuable advice.

I am strongly inclined toward option #3.

It is a dreadful shame that Winston Churchill never had the benefit of Molloy's expertise during World War II. Churchill might have been an effective leader and might even have proved an inspiring speaker during that period, had he either acquired a propellor-beanie to go with the bow ties he wore, or had he substituted the rep-stripe "regular" cravats that Molloy seems to be so fond of. Churchill even took to wearing jumpsuits. Molloy certainly wouldn't have stood still for that!

If people really are as idiotic as Molloy suggests, that they depend on somebody's necktie to determine whether or not they should be trusted, it seems to me we are all in trouble. But with all due respect, I believe the "expert" is wrong. People have learned over the years to respect and admire NBC News correspondent Irving R. Levine. Mr. Levine has worn a bow tie for as long as I can remember, and yet audiences have never confused him with Pee Wee Herman.

It would be a big mistake, I think, for Mr. Levine or me, or Mr. Herman for that matter, to affect some other kind of neckwear, just because John Molloy says it would make us more trusted. Would you trust Pee Wee Herman more if he wore a rep tie? Me neither.

By the way, for you guys who've asked me how to tie a bow tie, it's very simple. You put the tie around your neck and cross the ends over as if you were starting to tie your shoelaces. Then you hold one end up as if it were already tied, and with the other hand take the other end, loop it over the top and tuck it behind the end that you're holding up. Then you futz with it until it's straight.

Once you've learned to tie it you will find the bow tie has many advantages. For one thing, if you spill your soup, you won't get a big spot on your tie.

> *For those who have lusted to be honored and trusted,*
> *A bow tie, I say, doesn't hurt.*
> *It isn't your tie that most people will eye—*
> *It's the big soupstain there on your shirt.*

Hello?
Is Anybody There?

As somebody who spends a fair amount of his time talking into television cameras and radio microphones, I can tell you that we broadcasters have certain illusions about you viewers and listeners. For openers, we expect you listeners to listen and you viewers to view.

Anybody in a room with a television set on is by definition a viewer, and anybody in a room or car with a radio that's on is by definition a listener, although this does not always reflect the truth. A person in the same room with a book is not necessarily a reader, even if the book is open.

It is probably a good thing that those of us who are jabbering away at these inanimate objects in our studios cannot see what is happening at the receiving end. We imagine, of course, that we are talking to a real person, but that's not always the case. Sometimes you get up and walk right out of the room while I'm in the middle of a sentence, I'll bet, without so much as an "excuse me" or "by your leave" or "I'll be right back," or anything.

And sometimes, I'm sure, just when I'm getting to what I think is the good part of whatever it is I'm telling you about, you and somebody else start talking to each other as if I weren't there. This would be a bit disconcerting to me if I knew it, but mercifully I don't. Oblivious to the fact that you are not paying attention any more, I keep going.

So there I am, all dressed up in my bow tie, with my hair slicked down and everything, assuming that I have your rapt, undivided attention, while you are actually wrapping a package, looking at your mail, fixing a sandwich, or eating one, or dressing or undressing, or Lord knows what. If I actually could "see you on the radio," you could have me arrested for being a Peeping Tom.

I do not mean to suggest that this is all your fault. It is your living room and your television set, your car and your car radio, after all. And if we news people were half as fascinating as so many of us think we are, you'd listen to more of what we have to say.

John Robinson and Mark Levy of the University of Maryland have done some scholarly studies of how network television news reports are being taken in on the receiving end. According to them, most people miss about two-thirds of the main points of most stories. In other words, we network news people are batting about .333. That would be excellent if we were playing baseball. But this is another game altogether.

The late E. B. White warned writers that the average reader is in trouble about half the time. If Messrs. Robinson and Levy are right, the average TV news viewer is in trouble about two-thirds of the time. This is slightly discouraging if you happen to be in my line of work.

Sometimes you will lose your audience no matter what you do. The phone rings, or the doorbell, or there's an urgent call of nature. Calls of nature always seem to the callee to be more urgent than anything the President or Congress have been up to on a given day.

Robinson and Levy suggest, among other things, that news broadcasters stop assuming total concentration on the part of the audience. They think we should repeat important information in case the listener/viewer happens to be distracted the first time around. They think we should stop trying to pack so much information into so little airtime, and concentrate instead on making more sense. Too often, I'm afraid, we think we're making sense, but from the audience's point of view, we're not. The idea of making sense certainly makes sense to me. I wish I had thought of it before.

Great Grandma
Was a Witch

I have never been one of those people who stays up nights wondering about their "roots." The way I see it, we all have two parents, four grandparents, eight great-grandparents, and sixteen great-great-grandparents, and by the time you go back ten generations, three hundred years or so, you had 1,024 people walking around from whom you are directly descended. In any group of 1,024 people, you are likely to find a horse thief or two, which explains perhaps why there is a little horse thief in the best of us.

Which brings me to the Osgood family. Charles E. Osgood, the distinguished University of Illinois professor who pioneered the study of psychosemantics, once told me that he and I had to be related. And actor Tony Perkins and I must be kinfolk. His father was actor Osgood Perkins. Anybody whose first, last, or middle name is Osgood, is most likely a distant cousin of mine, I'm told. Over the years that I've been broadcasting I've heard from a number of Osgoods out there, wondering if I happen to be their long-lost uncle.

Somebody sent me a tattered old family Bible, recording several Osgood births, deaths, and marriages dating back to the early 1800s. It also shows that there were a few hookers in the family. That doesn't surprise me in the least.

Just recently I received a letter from a Connecticut Osgood, who had done some research on the Osgoods and had come across an old Osgood will. Now you're talking, I thought. Naturally, the idea of an Osgood bequest caught my attention right away. However, as it turned out, Peter Osgood of Upper Wallop, Hampshire, England, had neglected to leave me any real estate, or a dime for that matter, when he passed away four hundred years ago last January. Rather thoughtless of him, if you ask me. For a moment there, I had visions of repairing to my ancestral home in Upper Wallop. But in 1590, at a time when Shakespeare was cranking out his early plays, I guess people didn't appreciate radio and TV correspondents the way they do now. The old boy cut me off without a dime.

Of course, come to think of it, I do owe Peter Osgood something, since all the American Osgoods, myself included, are apparently descended from him. Peter's great-grandson, John Osgood, took off for the Massachusetts Bay in 1637, and settled in Andover, Mass. One offspring of John's and a possible ancestor of mine is Samuel Osgood, who was born in Andover, became a member of the Continental Congress, was a friend of George Washington's, and an organizer of two banks, one of which is now Citibank, and the other, Chase Manhattan. Given my own present relations with these very same banks, it does not seem very likely I could be descended from Samuel Osgood. Samuel was definitely not my kind of guy.

But there is another, even more intriguing possibility. John Osgood's daughter-in-law, Mary Clement Osgood, was indicted for witchcraft by the Salem grand jury in 1692. She confessed, according to the records, and escaped the gallows only because Cotton Mather, whose conscience must have gotten the better of him, persuaded her to recant her confession on October 19, 1692.

I could claim one or the other, but not both Samuel and Mary Clement Osgood, as ancestors, since they are in different branches of the family tree. But I'll tell you one thing. I would rather be descended from a witch than from a banker any old day.

The Hard Part

I have been asked to deliver commencement addresses at two different educational institutions this year. One is a full-fledged university in upstate New York, and the other is a grammar school about a block and a half from my house in New Jersey. I have thought about delivering exactly the same address to both graduating classes, even though the average age of one class will be twenty-one, and the average age of the other will be eleven. That is because what I have to say will be just as understandable to one group as it will to the other. What I want to say will be something like this:

It has been a very long time since I was twenty-one years old, and an even longer time since I was eleven, but I can remember both ages pretty well. When I was eleven, I was quite worried, because everybody told me that junior high school was going to be quite a bit more difficult than grammar school had been. From the seventh grade on, I had been warned, life would be real and earnest.

It turned out that junior high wasn't so tough after all, but I knew full well, because everybody told me, that high school would be quite another matter. Much more would be expected of me in high school, I was sure, and I was plenty worried about it, too. But it turned out to be nowhere near as bad as I had feared.

However, there was no question that college would be

difficult in the extreme. Colleges and universities would separate the men from the boys, and the women from the girls, I was informed. Well, I don't know about that, but at my college they did separate the boys from the girls and the men from the women. But the work still didn't seem as oppressive as advertised.

Still ahead of me lay other prospects: The military, which would straighten me out in a hurry, graduate school, which would be murderously difficult, or something called the "real world." In the "real world," you would have to go out and get a real job and do actual work.

In the army, it turned out, I was assigned to the U.S. Army Band. It was a dirty job, but somebody had to do it. Since then I have been working in the broadcasting business. At the local station they said it would be much harder work at the network. In radio they said it would be far more demanding in television. Turns out all of it is interesting work with hardly any heavy lifting or drudgery involved. In other words, I never *did* have to get a "real" job or do "actual" work.

When I was single, everybody said life gets tough after you get married. Then they told me having kids and family responsibilities and owning a home and paying taxes would wear me down. Hasn't happened yet.

Life is earnest, life is real,
Up to the very end.
And the hard part, everybody says,
Is just around the bend.
But here's a little secret that I want to share with you.
What is true for other people, need not be the case for you.
When they tell you that the hard part starts in just a little
     while,
Look worried, if you want to, but inside of you, just smile.

II

"AND TO THE REPUBLIC
FOR RICHARD STANDS..."

The Richard Stands Principle

Salespeople in computer stores have a certain priority in mind. Selling you something is on the list, but it is not right on the top. Top priority for a computer-store clerk is proving that he knows a great deal more about computers than you do. If he can prove that in the first five seconds, he can win the contest, and it doesn't matter whether he then sells you anything or not. In my case, it is easy for the salesclerk to win, because you don't have to know very much about computers at all to know more than I do.

I do own a personal computer, however, and have been trying to learn to write with it. I am a very old dog to be trying to learn such a new trick, admittedly, but I am nothing if not game. So I walked into the computer store, trying to assume a knowledgeable air, and asked the young man to tell me about modems.

He sneered the mandatory sneer and then asked the question he knew would gain him the immediate advantage.

"Do you have cereal in the face?" he inquired. I reached immediately up to my chin to see if a bit of dried oatmeal was there, an inadvertent souvenir of breakfast that morning.

"I don't *think* I have cereal in the face," I said. "Do I?"

It turned out that what he was saying was not "cereal in the face," but "serial interface." I would have preferred "cereal in the face," to tell you the truth, because at least

I know what that means. "Serial interface" is still a puzzle. When you don't understand what a phrase means, it often sounds like something you *do* understand. In spoken English, this is known as the Richard Stands principle.

Richard Stands is mentioned in no American history book, yet to countless schoolchildren over the years he has been a central figure in American life. Many is the schoolchild who each morning pledges allegiance, not only to the flag of the United States of America, but also to "the republic for Richard Stands." Never mind that you don't know who this Stands fellow is. You figure the teacher will get to that later in the year.

Richard Stands also shows up in many prayers. Stands himself does not appear, but his principle is much in evidence. In the Lord's Prayer, for example, "Our Father Who art in Heaven" is often asked to "lead us not into Penn Station." Some kids will say it that way for years, without ever questioning why Penn Station should be so singled out as a place not to be led into. And who knows how many kids believe that the Hail Mary begins: "Hail Mary full of grapes, the Lord is with thee."

It's easy for a child, or anyone else for that matter, to misunderstand something that has no connection to his everyday reality. For children, prayers, the pledge of allegiance, and other such esoteric collections of words fall into the category of mystical knowledge—something they don't have to understand now, but that will become clear some time later.

When some time later finally does arrive, most people either have come to understand, accept on faith, or ignore the things in the twilight zone of knowledge.

For my part, I have faith. I have faith that the cereal in the face will be compatible with my system or that the computer salesman will take pity on me, divine my true needs, and give me what it takes to keep on writing. Just tell me what cereal my computer prefers. I'll wear it, on my face or anywhere else it wants. This I understand! My kids like to eat cereal with me, though they don't require me to dribble it all over myself. Serial interface I don't know from.

Here, data banks, see the Captain Crunch on my chin? If that doesn't suit your tastes, we'll try the Cocoa Puffs tomorrow.

Sweeping Changes

Lawyers talk funny. They write funny, too. Legalese is like another language in which you and I become two other people: to wit, the Party of the First Part, and the Party of the Second Part. There has been an effort in recent years to get lawyers to use plain English, so that anybody could understand what a given contract, law, regulation, etc., was trying to say, radical a notion as that may be. Some government agencies have rewritten their regulations to make them clearer and easier to understand.

Poets and lawyers have exactly opposite intentions. Poets want to write so that their language is subtle and nuanced, rich with possible interpretations. Lawyers are supposed to write so that later (when somebody sues) there will be no question as to what was meant by a certain phrase. The ideal is that there should be only one possible meaning.

One way to unsnarl the convoluted gobbledygook of government is to make more use of simple, declarative sentences, omitting needless words. (See *The Elements of Style*, by Strunk and White). However, as Albert Einstein once pointed out, you should make things as simple as possible, but not simpler. There is such a thing as omitting one word too many.

The U.S. International Trade Commission omitted three words too many. In trying to streamline its regulations, the ITC took an editor's pencil to the section that deals with the importing of brooms made of corn bristles. To protect the American corn-broom industry, there were restrictions and heavy tariffs on brooms made "wholly or partly from broom corn." The words "wholly or partly" seemed unnecessary, and so in the revised edition, out they went. In trying to sweep away the extra words, however, the ITC may have swept away the business.

Recently, the Customs Service was asked whether, under the new language, a broom with 28 percent to 43 percent corn bristles would be subject to the tariffs and import limitations. The answer was no.

In other words, broommakers in Mexico, let us say, can now stuff their brooms with cheap materials, use a lot of vegetable fibers or grass, and still market their products here in the U.S. as corn brooms, competing with the fifty or so American broom companies, and selling their brooms for about half what a quality U.S. maker would have to charge for the real McCoy. "It's absolutely unbelievable," says one broommaker. "It's thrown our industry in turmoil!" says another. There are some fifty American companies making roughly twenty million corn brooms a year. Floor brooms, whisk brooms. All sorts of brooms.

Although Congress went along with the word changes, there's now an effort being made on Capitol Hill to correct what was obviously an error. The folks who re-wrote the regulations never intended to say what the words ended up saying. David B. Beck, a Commission official, has written a letter to the Customs people, saying: "The consequences this would have on the tariff treatment of these products were never brought to our attention when we could have done something about it."

Senator Lloyd Bentsen, D-Texas, is pushing for legislation to do something about it, to re-re-write the regulations. Representative Terry Bruce, D-Illinois, is doing the same thing in the House.

The moral is: It's a good idea to make language simple. But don't make it *too* simple.

Defining Your Terms

Some of the simplest everyday things turn out to be not so simple when you try to define them. Everybody knows what "time" is, for example. But if your life depended on coming up with a clear definition of time, you would be in a lot of trouble.

In the news, there are plenty of references to "terrorists." But anybody who tries to spell out what is meant by the word "terrorist" runs into difficulty. We all know what a terrorist is, but the United Nations has been unable to come up with a working definition. The State Department and the Pentagon have different definitions, and at least one congressional committee finally decided that there is no way of defining the word "terrorist" without making value judgments that not everybody is going to agree with. One man's "terrorist" is another's "freedom fighter." It's impossible to pass laws against terrorism if you can't spell out with some precision what it is you are talking about.

Definitions are important in the law, of course. In Wilmington, Delaware, right now, there is a big legal battle being fought in the U.S. District Court. Several giant cookie-baking companies are fighting over the recipe for so-called "dual textured" cookies.

That means cookies that are crispy on the outside and soft and chewy on the inside. Procter & Gamble Co. claims it discovered the process, patented it in 1983, and that Nabisco has infringed the patent.

Nabisco, Keebler Co., and Frito-Lay claim that they were making cookies that were crispy on the outside and chewy on the inside *before* P&G got its patent. So the Nabisco, Keebler, and Frito-Lay lawyers asked Procter & Gamble to define their terms. Among the terms they wanted defined were "cookie" and "dough."

Now, I know what the word cookie means and so do you. My two-year-old, Jamie, knows what a cookie is and can ask for it by name. But the definition turns out to be so important in this case that here are these high-priced lawyers, these learned counsellors, asking the judge, Joseph Longobardi, to please tell them what a cookie is, and what dough is.

Judge Longobardi is not a man who shies away from an intellectual exercise, but he declined to oblige the opposing lawyers in their request.

"It should not be the Court's burden to supply definitions of the terms," he told them in a memo.

If a wise jurist like Judge Longobardi doesn't want to have to render definitions for such relatively simple concepts as cookie and dough, no wonder the U.N. can't get together on more controversial matters.

> *If we truly don't know*
> *The meaning of "dough"*
> *If "cookie" is something mysterious,*
> *It is surely no wonder*
> *We so often blunder*
> *When we're dealing with matters more serious.*

Greeting Cards

The greeting-card industry has discovered a terrible, wonderful thing. Terrible for us, wonderful for them. What they have discovered is that we Americans don't know how to write letters any more. It could be argued that we don't know how to write *anything* any more. But what makes this terrible thing such a wonderful thing for the greeting-card business, is that people now not only depend on greeting cards to say Happy Birthday and Happy Anniversary, but they also need pre-printed messages to handle every other conceivable situation that might arise in life.

It started, I suppose, with the specialized cards. "Happy Birthday to My Wonderful Mother-in-Law." "Get Well Soon, My Favorite Uncle." From there, it sort of branched out, as the card companies realized that the public wanted to use cards instead of letters.

I can see them now, in the creative departments of Hallmark and American Greetings, frantically trying to anticipate occasions that might have called for a note in the old days, and therefore require a card in these new days. Such as:

> *"I'm terribly sorry I did what I did,*
> *And I'm sorry I said what I said.*

You really are not such a terrible kid,
And I shouldn't have told you 'drop dead.' "

Only occasionally would such a message be appropriate, but occasionally is apparently often enough for the card companies to make a decent living. As a writer of doggerel myself, I'm encouraged to imagine a whole new market for unlikely couplets. How about:

"Please don't call the sheriff and send me to jail,
I swear on my honor the check's in the mail."

Or,

"Roses are red, violets are blue,
I wouldn't try to start my car if I were you."

Or,

"My darling, this is hard for me, it really does upset me,
But I cannot see you any more, because my wife won't let
me."

Life, in its rich and abundant variety, gives rise to an infinite number of possible circumstances, so the companies will have to make, and the stores will have to carry, an enormous stock of cards. Cards from the young to the old. Cards from the old to the young. Cards of acceptance and rejection, cards of love and anger and hate and fear and every other known human emotion. Even love letters for lawyers.

"Whereas and henceforth, and notwithstanding the above,
The undersigned does stipulate that you're the one I love."

It will take computers, of course, to keep track of all the various situational messages, and Lord knows we need things to keep computers busy. If a poor friend of yours has an exceptional piece of good luck, you could consult the data bank under friend, poor, luck, good . . . and come up with:

> *"I hear that no more do you lack certain pottery.*
> *Congratulations on winning the lottery."*

The message on the card might not exactly fit the circumstances. In that case, you'll have to settle for something vague:

> *"Hello and how are you, I just want to say,*
> *I really must run now, but have a nice day."*

It's the price you pay for convenience.

Words to Live By

There are traps in the English language that are more easily fallen into than gotten out of. One of these is to get so bogged down in the so-called rules that you make it difficult for the person on the receiving end to understand what you are talking about.

At the beginning of every broadcast day, I sign on. At the end, I sign off. There is much work to be done in between. On radio alone there are twenty-one broadcasts a week to be turned out. Each of these has a number of sentences that it's composed of. Words are what each sentence is made up of. What order should these words be put in?

There is a violation of the writing rules which I admit I am frequently guilty of. It is a trap that is easy to fall into. However, it is one that I do not worry much about. Ending a sentence with a preposition is what I am referring to. The astute reader may discover several instances of what I'm talking about in the very piece you are now looking at. Ending a sentence with a preposition is considered okay where I come from. (Some may feel that wherever I come from I should go back to.) Recently I ended a sentence with a preposition, realizing full well that a preposition is what some people think you should *never*, under any circumstances, end a sentence with. Such people I'm sick to death of, fed up with, and put off by.

If terminal prepositionalism is an error, it is one that there is plenty of distinguished precedent for. Winston Churchill was once taken to task for ending one of his elegant sentences with a preposition and his withering reply was: "This is the sort of arrant pedantry up with which I will not put."

With me, it all depends on the mood I'm in. Sometimes I don't write sentences that you would want to put a preposition at the end of. Other times the caboose position is the one the little preposition seems to cry out for.

I remember reading somewhere the observation that Pittsburgh is a bad city to get something in your eye in. However, it was pointed out, Pittsburgh happens to be a very good city to get something in your eye out in. This is perfectly logical, since a city people often get something in their eyes in would have a lot of experience in getting things people have gotten in their eyes out.

The placement of prepositions in sentences is not the sort of issue that gets me all riled up. In fact, the people who fuss about such things are the ones I get mad at. There's a story they tell at Harvard University about a visitor to the campus who asks, "Excuse me, but would you be good enough to tell me where the Widener Library is at?"

"Sir," was the sneering reply, "at Harvard we do not end a sentence with a preposition."

"Well, in that case, forgive me," said the visitor. "Permit me to rephrase my question. Would you be good enough to tell me where the Widener Library is at, jackass?"

I think that pretty well sums it up.

Read My Eyes,
Not My Lips

This is the age of "your lips tell me *yes, yes,* but there's *no, no* in your eyes."

Just think about it. You used to be able to tell what people were thinking by listening to what they said. Nowadays, for one reason or another, many people will tell you one thing while they are thinking exactly the opposite.

You ask the boss for a raise or a promotion, for example, giving him the full sales pitch about how long it's been and how much you've been contributing these days.

And what he tells you is that the home office has put a freeze on raises and promotions just now, but that as soon as the right opportunity presents itself, he'll do everything he can to see that you get what you've got coming.

While he is saying this, however, his face and tone of voice are saying:

"You know what I hate about this job? It's having to listen to whiners like you. Why don't you just go back and do your job and stop complaining. Go away and leave me alone!"

We are trained not to say unpleasant things to each other, so the words may come out sounding polite and civilized enough. But watch the face.

"I'd love to go out with you tonight, George," says Cybil, "but I have to wash my hair."

Meanwhile her face and tone of voice are saying: "Get out of my life, creep. I wouldn't go out with you if you were the last man on earth."

Three classic lines are:

"You're looking great!"

"It was swell running into you!"

"Let's have lunch!"

Meanwhile, the face and eyes are saying:

"God, she looks like death warmed over."

"Just my luck to run into this turkey when I'm running late."

"Let me out of here!"

It's almost as if one believed that someday a higher court would be reading a transcript of the conversation, in which all the words would be taken at face value, and the facial expressions and tone of voice completely removed.

"See, Your Honor? I did *not* tell the plaintiff to 'go stuff it.' All I told him to do was to 'have a nice day.' "

It's not what you say, but the way that you say it.

If you are such an accomplished dissembler that you can think one thing and say another with your words and voice and facial expressions all at the same time, then I would say there is only one vocation for you—and I am not referring to the used-car or aluminum-siding business.

A person with your gifts and inclinations is ideally suited for the U.S. Congress.

%@*&#

Gosh! I just found out the doggondest thing! Did you realize that obscene language is on the way out? I sure as heck didn't. Golly Ned! I would not have guessed that on my own, to tell you the truth. Gee, the decline of obscenity sure hasn't turned up yet in the kind of conversation that I have occasion to hear every day. In fact I would have guessed that obscene language was replacing regular ordinary language as the standard means of communication. But an English professor at Cleveland State University, William Chisholm, is on record as saying that the doggone pendulum is now swinging away from dirty words and toward good old-fashioned respect and decency. Well, I'll be a son of a gun!

Shucks! To hear the professor tell it, foul and filthy language has become so prevalent and commonplace in our society that nobody is really shocked and disgusted any more. If you are not going to shock and disgust people, there is simply no point in talking like that.

I must admit that the logic of this sounds to me a lot like that of Yogi Berra when somebody asked him about a certain restaurant. "Nobody eats there any more," said Berra, "it's too crowded." Well, if the reason nobody is cussing any more is that cussing is too prevalent, then *somebody* must be using the bad words. Maybe people are just hearing tape recordings of bad words actually spoken in the

1960s at the height of the so-called "free speech" movement. Or the famous White House tapes that President Nixon made during the Watergate days. I don't think so, though. If the professor means that the words are still being used but without the intended shock value, or without any value whatsoever, I would go along with him there.

Another scholar, Reinhold Ahman, who edits some darn publication called *Maledicta: The Journal of Verbal Aggression*, swears that there are no strong swear words left any more. You can go to your neighborhood theater or tune in on your neighborhood cable TV channel and hear Eddie Murphy or Richard Pryor say exactly the same words that got Lenny Bruce thrown into jail not that many years ago.

Now, nobody seems to give a hoot. We have heard all the four-letter words too much and in every conceivable variation. Some people who have no idea what a noun is, will insert a profanity before every noun, as in: "Pass the %@*&# salt, please."

Others display amazing ingenuity as to obscenity placement. Would you think it possible to insert a profanity in the very middle of an adverb? The answer is "abso%$#@&-lutely."

Mind Over Mouth

We have a habit of saying whatever pops into our heads. This gives our speech a refreshing candor and spontaneity, but sometimes it gets us into trouble.

We often engage our tongues without putting our brains into gear.

Lee Townsend, the editor of *The CBS Evening News*, came back to work only weeks after suffering a heart attack. One of his bosses, surprised to see him back so soon, shook his hand and said what popped into his head, which was, "Well, Lee, you don't look a day older." Lee smiled and said, "I almost wasn't."

That's one of those lines almost everybody wishes he'd said, but I suppose it's not worth having a heart attack just to be in a position to say it.

There is no calling words back once they're out there, and verbal shooting from the hip is a difficult habit to break. It seems to me pipe smokers have a distinct advantage over the rest of us in this regard. When pressed for a fast response, a pipe smoker can always pause to puff once or twice or relight the pipe. This creates an impression of thoughtfulness and, indeed, it does give him a chance to think for a moment or two.

James Schlesinger, the former secretary of everything, is the master of the pipe pause. Nobody seems to mind the wait as long as they have something to watch while they are waiting. In this case, they get to watch a man lighting his pipe.

A cigarette can be used for the same purpose, but it doesn't take long enough to light a cigarette. And since cigarettes hardly ever go out, you can't always relight one to give yourself time to think. Talking without thinking is like swallowing without chewing.

What we need is the equivalent of fletcherizing. Fletcherizing means chewing your food a lot before you swallow. A man by the name of Horace Fletcher, in a book called *The ABC's of Nutrition*, wrote at the turn of the century that every mouthful of food should be chewed at least thirty-two times before being swallowed. It got to be such a big fad in this country that the verb "to fletcherize" came into common use. Fletcher believed that since we have thirty-two teeth, we should chew thirty-two times, once for each tooth.

John D. Rockefeller and Thomas Edison were among those who subscribed to Fletcher's theory, which must have made them fascinating companions at the dinner table. If it was their turn to talk while only ten chews into a mouthful of food, you'd have to wait for twenty-two more chews before they could say whatever they had to say.

By that time, somebody had probably changed the subject. Come to think of it, Rockefeller made some pretty shrewd moves in his day and Edison came up with some pretty bright ideas himself.

It only goes to prove what I've always said: You can't talk and think at the same time.

Aye, AI

As you are probably aware by now, Artificial Intelligence (AI) is what the computer whizzes are working on now. Pretty soon, they say, computers will be able to learn from their mistakes, the way people do. Once they have made a mistake, they will absorb it somehow and never make that particular mistake again. This is quite different from us human beings, of course, who keep making exactly the same mistakes over and over again.

The trouble with developing a machine with Artificial Intelligence (AI) based on Human Intelligence (HI), is that Human Intelligence (HI) only accounts for a small part of the progress of our species. It seems to me that Human Stupidity (HS) has also played a key role.

Take Christopher Columbus. On his famous voyages, Columbus had the wrong idea completely about where he was headed. When he got here, he had no idea where he was. Then when he got back home, he had no idea where he had been. But today nobody holds this against him. The world owes a great debt to Columbus's ignorance and intransigence. People tried to talk some sense into him, but he wouldn't listen.

Time and time again, history has demonstrated the value of dumb luck (DL), but until recently nobody has tried to reproduce DL electronically. There is a young man in

Geneva, New York, however, who claims to be working on a computer that will play chess *badly*. In a speech last summer to the Instrument Society of America, Michael Ferris said he would program the computer with a set of human-style excuses. IDMBH ("I did my best, honest!") would include such standard responses as IDKYWIT ("I didn't know you wanted it today.") and TDEI ("The dog erased it.").

Ferris is on to something, I believe. Perhaps the only reason nobody has pursued so obvious a goal as Artificial Stupidity (AS) is that there seems to be such an abundant world supply of the real thing. Ferris should keep at it, though. Someday, a shortage of Human Stupidity and Stubbornness (HSS) may develop and he will be ready with Artificial Stupidity and Stubbornness (ASS) to fill the void.

Cosmic Illiteracy

The word "illiteracy" used to mean not knowing how to read
or write. Then functional illiteracy came along. Functional
illiteracy means not being able to read or write well enough
to function. Functionally illiterate people can't make any
sense of what they read, and nobody else can make sense
of what they write. There's an awful lot of that going around.

In recent years we've been hearing about other kinds
of illiteracy as well. The National Geographic Society has
pointed out that American students on the high school level,
and even on the college level, are often geographic illiterates.
They don't know where any place is. One college professor
sent me papers turned in by his sophomore class. The students had been given blank maps, and they were supposed
to pinpoint the location of several places. One student had
Cuba in the South Pacific. Another put New Zealand in the
North Atlantic. Few were able to place Vietnam anywhere
near its actual location. Honest.

There's a corresponding historical illiteracy, according
to history teachers. Young people today seem to think that
before the Vietnam War, nothing much of consequence happened in the world. They don't know who Alexander the
Great was, or Peter the Great, or why they were so great.
They can't tell you about the Magna Carta or the Mayflower
Compact, or the Monroe Doctrine. When it comes to the

great human events of the past, they haven't the foggiest who anybody is, what he did, or when.

Math teachers recently complained of mathematical illiteracy. "Innumeracy," as one of them called it. Seems many Americans have a great aversion to mathematics in any form, and when they encounter numbers their scalps begin to itch and their teeth begin to ache. Never mind calculus or trigonometry. There are college kids today who couldn't do long division if their lives depended on it. Lord help them if the batteries on their electronic calculators run down.

Now for something completely different: Cosmic illiteracy. A survey was done by researchers at MIT and Northern Illinois University, and 1,100 American adults were asked basic questions about the universe, such as: "Is the sun a planet, a star, or something else?"

Twenty-five percent answered that the sun is a planet. Fifteen percent said it was something else. Five percent didn't even take a stab at an answer. Only 55 percent, slightly more than half, knew that the sun is a star. Is the universe expanding? Seventy-five percent of American adults didn't know that it is. MIT Professor Alan Lightman, co-author of the study, says that there is apparently a psychological need for people to believe in a static universe. "Many feel uncomfortable with a universe that is moving and changing," he says. Will the sun eventually burn itself out? Only 37 percent said yes. Granted, there is no need to panic about the sun burning out, to quit your job, or cancel your Saturday-night date or anything. Best guess is the sun won't fizzle out for another ten billion years or so. Even so, Professor Lightman finds it shocking that so many of us are "cosmic illiterates."

"Only a third of American adults have a minimally acceptable understanding of the universe," he says. In other words, most of us don't know our asteroids from our elbows.

The one encouraging thing in the survey is that the younger the respondents, the more they seem to know about the sun, the moon, the planets, and the stars. Many older people tend to feel that it's no skin off their noses if the universe is expanding or not, since there's not much they can do about it anyway.

Knowledge, unfortunately, is finite. It is ignorance that knows no bounds.

The Perfect Face

Some people want to quantify everything. Words bother them. They like numbers better. Numbers seem more businesslike and objective somehow. Numbers are more useful; you can measure, count, and weigh with them. You can punch them into a calculator and add and subtract, multiply and divide them. You can put them in a computer and analyze the daylights out of them until you are blue in the face.

Numbers are, therefore, very popular in the business world where the "bottom line" is so all-fired important. Of course, if any of the numbers are wrong, everything including the number on the bottom line will be wrong, too. Nevertheless, there is a constant effort to reduce everything to numbers so that it *can* be analyzed to death. Chances are your boss is a numbers person. The numbers people have taken over the world.

Perhaps this explains why I have not taken over the world. I am decidedly not a numbers person. There are many things in this world that should not be quantified, in my opinion. It may be possible to reduce something beautiful to numbers, but you lose something when you do.

For example, at the University of Louisville, psychologist Michael Cunningham has come up with a way to define feminine pulchritude. I'm not talking about 36-24-36. I am talking about faces here. Cunningham asked students to rate twenty-six "attractiveness characteristics" of fifty women, twenty-seven of whom were finalists in the Miss Universe contest. Based on the responses from 150 students, he devised his technical formula expressing the ideal of beauty.

In words, one might describe the eyes as shining, or liquid, or sparkling, deep or bright or almond-shaped. One soulful look from a woman with beautiful eyes can knock a man right off his feet. But Cunningham has got it all worked out in numbers. The eye width, he says, should be three-tenths the width of the face and the visible eyeball should be one-fourteenth the distance between the hairline and the tip of the chin.

In words, you might describe a woman's nose as aquiline or upturned, pert or button. But what's important in the numbers formula is that the nose should be less than 5 percent of the area of the face. Six percent, she's got a big nose.

The mouth, according to the University of Louisville formulation, should be 50 percent of the width of the face measured at mouth level. More than 50 percent is too big. Less than 50 percent is, apparently, too small to be ideal. The chin length should be 20 percent of the height of the face.

It certainly is good to have all this expressed in manageable terms. Beauty is not in the eye of the beholder after all: It is in the numbers. Now that this numerical assessment has been done, it will be of enormous value to any red-blooded young man in assessing his most romantic feelings. All he needs is a tape measure and a set of calipers.

"How do I love thee?" the poet asks. As soon as I can give you some precise measurements for the depth and breadth and height my soul can reach, I'll let you know.

Surveys

Almost every day there are new surveys out telling us how this or that group feels about this or that subject, from foreign policy to underarm deodorants. One would get the impression that there's been a huge buildup in the army of nose counters out there counting our noses.

But tell the truth now, has any survey ever actually surveyed you? Have they ever knocked on your door, or called you on the phone, or stopped you on the street to inquire about your preferences in soap or politicians? No? Doesn't that make you feel sort of left out?

Has anybody in your family ever been polled or surveyed? How about your friends? Have any of them ever been included in, say, a TV ratings sample? Let me take it a step further. Have you ever met anybody who has been polled?

If the answer to all these questions is no, then you are like me. I have never been polled or surveyed, and neither has anybody in my family or any of my friends or anybody I ever met. I thought I was being polled one time, but it turned out the guy on the phone was trying to trick me into buying aluminum siding.

But somebody must be answering all these pollsters' questions. The news is full of surveys about everything under the sun. (The Lincoln Nebraska *Star* recently ran a survey indicating that, for whatever it's worth, Nebraska Republicans are much more likely than Nebraska Democrats to sleep in the nude.)

Since so many political and business judgments are made these days on the basis of what the polls and surveys say people think, I decided to do a little survey survey of my own. The results break down as follows:

	Yes	No	Get Lost
Do you ever watch television?	75%	0%	25%
Have you ever been polled about television?	0%	75%	25%
Do you ever listen to the radio?	75%	0%	25%
Do you ever eat food?	75%	0%	25%
Has any survey ever asked you about food?	0%	75%	25%
Do you ever use soap?	75%	0%	25%
Have you ever been polled about soap?	0%	75%	25%
Do you have any opinions?	75%	0%	25%
Has any pollster ever asked for your opinions?	0%	75%	25%
Do you believe in surveys?	75%	0%	25%
Do you believe in the tooth fairy?	0%	0%	100%

Professional research people will probably scoff at my methods. They will argue that four people in McGlade's Bar on a Friday afternoon is not a valid statistical sample. The margin of error in my poll, by the way, is ±100%.

For the record, though: Just because neither you nor anybody else you know has ever seen or heard something with your own eyes or ears does not necessarily mean the thing does not exist. And just because a large number of people happen to believe something, it does not necessarily follow that the thing is true.

Nothing But the Tooth

Recently, I made a kidding reference to the Tooth Fairy. In a mock survey to find out how many of us actually have been polled by the pollsters, I asked: "Do you believe in the Tooth Fairy?" Of our sample of four people at McGlade's Bar, you may recall, 0% said they did.

It never occurred to me that somebody in real life might have actually done a survey about the Tooth Fairy, but it turns out somebody has. In a recent issue of *American Health* magazine there is a report done by Dr. Marvin Berman, a pediatric dentist from Chicago.

It figures that a pediatric dentist would have more than the usual degree of interest in the subject of the Tooth Fairy, and particularly the Fairy's fee structure. Dr. Berman wanted to find out how much money is being left under kids' pillows in exchange for a tooth these days.

He reports that one dollar is now the going rate. When I was a kid, twenty-five cents was the standard. Berman says the average was twelve cents at the turn of the century, and fifty-six cents in the 1960s.

To me, this does not have the ring of authenticity to it. Can you imagine anybody leaving twelve cents or fifty-six cents under a kid's pillow? I can't. I figure it was a dime for a while, then went up to a quarter, then half a dollar, and now it's got nowhere to go but *two* dollars, or maybe *five*.

You can see that inflation has come to the bizarre world of the Tooth Fairy. It's really been putting the bite on the old boy. Or is the Tooth Fairy a girl?

We don't have a very clear picture of the Tooth Fairy in our heads. We know what Santa Claus looks like. We've seen lots of pictures of the Easter Bunny. But there seems no definitive notion of what the Tooth Fairy is supposed to look like, dress like, or act like. We don't know where he's supposed to live. There are no legends about how he gets around, or how he gets into the house. All we know is that he has this mighty strange obsession with kids' teeth, and this peculiar habit of turning up in the middle of the night to pay cash on the barrelhead . . . under the pillow, I mean.

Even as a child I used to wonder what in the world the Tooth Fairy was supposed to do with the teeth once he took them. What use could he or anybody else possibly have for so many millions of useless little teeth? Is it just an odd hobby? Or is the Tooth Fairy building something, a monumental structure out of baby teeth? Dr. Berman says in the old days the Fairy would leave more cash if the tooth had been pulled than he would if the thing just fell out. "I think the Fairy feels guilty sometimes," Berman says.

I don't know why the silly Fairy should feel guilty. I mean *he* didn't pull the doggone tooth, did he? All I know is that at a dollar a throw, maintaining the Tooth Fairy tradition gets a bit expensive when you have five little kids.

About the only positive thing I can think of to say about the Tooth Fairy is that he is relatively unexploited so far. The card companies and toy companies have not yet figured out a way to make a lot of money off the Tooth Fairy the way they have off Santa or the Bunny. No doubt they would do it in a minute if they could think of some way. They'll come up with something, I'm sure.

Or maybe they think of the Tooth Fairy as an idea that is so sweet and innocent, so fine and noble, that they would never do anything so crass as to try to make a buck out of it. If you believe that, you must believe in the Tooth Fairy.

Deer Hunters

I have had the wrong idea about deer hunters, and about deer-hunting accidents. I've always thought that almost all the injuries suffered in such accidents were caused by hunters shooting at each other by mistake. During the deer-hunting season there are often news stories about deer hunters somehow mistaking each other for deer, although it has never seemed to me that the deer and the deer hunters bore much resemblance to each other.

The deer have four legs, for one thing. Furthermore, the deer never dress themselves up in bright red shirts or jackets. The problem seems to be that anything that moves out there in the woods stands a fairly good chance of being shot at. During the season some farmers have taken to writing the word "COW" in large letters on their cows, so that the hunters will know they are not looking at a herd of particularly fat lactating deer, standing there in a pasture all facing the same direction and waiting for somebody to come and shoot them.

Nevertheless, there are hazards out there, other than hunters' weapons. Guns don't kill people. Trees kill people. It turns out that during the season, it is not only apples and leaves that fall from the trees. It is deer hunters. A study has recently been released showing that, statistically, over a third of deer-hunting accidents are caused by hunters falling out of trees. This may sound absurd on the face of it, but the Centers for Disease Control looked at deer hunting–accident figures provided by the state of Georgia, and concluded that tree stands, the elevated perches from which hunters wait for deer to come by, accounted for 214 of the 594 deer-hunting accidents reported.

Some of the tree stands are platforms, on which you stand. It's easier to stand on a platform than on a tree limb. Others are chairs in which you sit. Sitting is almost always easier than standing. Both kinds are balanced on the boughs of trees. If the bough breaks, the tree stand will fall, and down will come hunter, weapon and all. According to the study the average distance of the fall was sixteen feet. You can hurt yourself rather badly falling sixteen feet. Especially if, as happened in twenty-seven of the cases, your gun accidentally goes off when you hit the ground.

Why did the hunters fall? Most of them simply lost their balance, although some had more exotic explanations. Eleven of them say they fell asleep up there. Waiting in a tree for a deer to show up can be a bit tiring, I guess. Eight of the hunters who fell had apparently been drinking. Either they admitted that or the game officials who found them came to that conclusion.

Forty of the hunters fell while climbing up trees. Forty-nine of them fell while climbing down. Two-thirds of the hunters who fell had never taken a hunting-safety course, and not one of them was wearing a safety harness.

One woman who had safely climbed up and safely put her tree stand into place, waited safely for a deer to come along. One did, and she shot it. The wounded deer, apparently figuring out where the bullet had come from, charged into the tree and it shook the hunter loose and she fell, breaking a leg. Pretty unsporting of that deer, if you ask me.

Rx Prayer

There is now some scientific evidence in support of the idea that sick people benefit when other people pray for them. I know that doesn't *sound* so scientific. But JAMA, *The Journal of the American Medical Association*, has now printed a summary of a study that was published last July in the *Southern Medical Journal*, indicating that hospitalized heart patients do better when somebody petitions the Almighty on their behalf.

The test was done as if prayer were a new product by some pharmaceutical company. In 1982 and 1983 three hundred and ninety-three patients at San Francisco General Medical Center's coronary care unit were assigned randomly, either to an experimental group that some born-again Christians would pray for, or to a control group that wasn't prayed for, at least not by these particular born-again Christians. The people who did the praying didn't meet the patients; they were given only first names and diagnoses, and were updated on the patients' condition from time to time.

It was a "double-blind" experiment. The patients who were being prayed for and those not being prayed for had no way of knowing whether they were in the prayed-for group or the not-prayed-for group. Also, the doctor who ran the experiment, Dr. Randolph Byrd, was kept in the dark about who was in which group until all the data had been recorded. This is important, because some might argue Dr. Byrd was predisposed to believing in the power of prayer in the first place. He's now off in Asia somewhere doing Christian missionary work. But at the time of the experiment, he was at the University of California, San Francisco. Dr. John Thompson, the editor of the *Southern Medical Journal*, says the prayer experiment, as it was conducted, meets all the scientific standards for testing, although he says he would like to see some further studies done, since the results of this one are so intriguing.

Although the patients were all equally sick when they checked into the hospital, the half who were prayed for had fewer episodes of congestive heart failure later, or pneumonia or cardiac arrest. In the control group, those not prayed for, twelve patients needed tubes inserted for breathing or feeding. In the prayed-for group, no tubes were needed. Nine control-group patients needed antibiotics, only two in the prayed-for group. Fifteen percent of the control group needed diuretics, only five percent of the patients who were prayed for. As far as most other possible complications were concerned, one group did about as well as the other. And since the pray-ers and pray-ees didn't know each other and nobody knew whether he or she was in one group or the other, it can't be the psychological boost from just knowing that did the trick.

There are some in the medical fraternity who think the whole idea of a prayer experiment is pure nonsense. Dr. Steven Kreisman of Gaston Memorial Hospital in Gastonia, North Carolina, complains that, "It's an attempt to return medicine to the Dark Ages, and to reduce physicians to the same status as witch doctors and faith healers." But Dr. Thompson thinks anything that helps patients get well is valid. Besides, he says, prayer is "about as benign a form of treatment as there is. There is no danger whatsoever."

In other words, as they say about chicken soup, "It couldn't hurt!"

You Figure It Out

If you're like most people, you've got too much to do and not enough time to do it. And this week, like so many others in the year, has been a long and hard one. You've taken care of the daily duties, handled the major and minor crises at work and at home. Maybe you've even taken some work home. You're exhausted, thoroughly drained. You need a mental health day to recuperate, so you ask the boss for a day off.

He says no and gives you the following explanation: There are 365 days in the year, but you take weekends off, so you have to subtract 104 days. That leaves you with 261 working days.

But you only work eight hours a day. The other sixteen you are either sleeping or tending to your own business. So you have to subtract another 174 days. That leaves eighty-seven.

But wait. We're not through subtracting yet. You eat lunch every day, and although lunch hours vary, it is estimated that the average worker consumes forty-five work days per year at lunch.

Coffee breaks? Figure twenty-one days over the course of the year. Take those twenty-one days from the forty-two left from the last calculation, and that leaves you twenty-one days to get your work done.

From those twenty-one days, you have to subtract your two weeks vacation. Ten work days. Continuing the subtraction, ten from twenty-one leaves you only eleven actual full work days in the entire year.

But, of course, you do not work on Christmas, New Year's, Independence Day, or Thanksgiving. Most firms now allow ten paid holidays per year. After subtracting the ten paid holidays from the eleven days remaining, you've got *one* full work day to your credit, and you want to take that day off? Forget it!

The boss sees no reason why you should be unduly exhausted given the above schedule. So, you explain to him that the U.S. population is 200 million or so, of whom 72 million are over the standard 65 year retirement age. That leaves 128 million people to do all the work.

If you subtract the 75 million under the age of 21, you're left with 53 million actual workers. Of that 53 million, 27,471,002 are employed by the federal government. That leaves 25,528,998 workers for all other jobs.

Subtracting the 8 million people who serve in the Armed Forces leaves us with 17,828,998 workers. From here we must turn to the city and state work force. Subtracting their 16,520,000 from 17,528,998 brings us down to 1,008,998.

Of course, we should also consider those people who have a complete aversion to work. It's been estimated that there are some 800,500 vagrants, bums, and the like. Now we're down to 208,498 people to carry the workload for the entire nation. But, you still have to subtract the prison population, which accounts for 208,496 people.

This means that two people are carrying everybody else. You know who those two are, don't you? It's you and me. No wonder we're so exhausted!

Fast Money

These days, information travels literally at the speed of light: 186,000 miles per second. In a flash, some event that takes place in one part of the world is known and reacted to in other far distant parts. I have noticed, however, that some kinds of information seem to move a lot faster than others.

For example, I use a personal computer now to pay my bills. I simply call into the bank using the computer modem, punch in the information about whom I want to pay, when, and how much, and Presto . . . the money is gone from my account the instant I push the Return key. It's wonderful. Banks have been transferring funds electronically for *years* now. They can make money disappear from your account with dazzling speed.

When you make a deposit, however, it's a different story. As the bank patiently explains to anybody who wonders about this, the check you deposit has to clear first. If it's an out-of-town check, this can take a long, long time. Never mind electronics. Apparently there is still an old gentleman with a green eyeshade and sleeve garters who is in charge of getting the money *into* your account. He uses an old-fashioned ledger book, into which he scribbles with a quill pen after dipping the quill into an antique inkwell. This slows things down, because he has to wait for the ink to dry. The money itself is loaded onto a very slow boat (hence the banking term "float") for shipment. The boat apparently makes several stops en route.

A similar differential exists when it comes to prices of consumer goods. A couple of earthquakes and a drought in Central and South America produced instant and dramatic increases in the price of coffee. No sooner does Juan Valdez notice that his coffee plants aren't doing so well than a clerk starts putting new price tags on the supermarket shelves.

Some years ago when OPEC announced a big oil-price hike, I reported the news on the radio and got in my car to drive home. On Route 4, just over the George Washington Bridge, the gas station attendant was already posting crayoned signs on the gasoline pumps reflecting the new price.

"What are you doing?" I asked him.

"Haven't you heard?" exclaimed the gas station man. "They just had it on the radio. OPEC has raised the price of crude oil."

Amazing how fast that sort of news travels. Subsequently, of course, OPEC had to *cut* prices because of the oil *glut*. We reported this on the radio, too, but the gas station man on Route 4 told me it would take a long time before that affected the price at the pump. Something to do with how long it takes that crude oil to be shipped (by slow tanker) to the refinery for processing and all that.

When it comes to prices, be it coffee, oil, or any other commodity, a strange variation of Newton's law applies. Things go *up* a lot faster than they come down.

Brother, Can You Spare Three Trillion Dollars?

The United States is the biggest debtor country in the world. Right now, the U.S. government owes roughly three trillion dollars ($3,000,000,000,000.00). That's three thousand billion. Or three million million, if that makes it any easier to fathom. Yes folks, you're right. That sure is one heck of a lot of money.

This is not to say that the United States is a poor country. Just because you owe a whole lot of money it doesn't mean that you are poor. Rich people and rich corporations often borrow money when they have something particularly expensive they want to do, such as buy a Van Gogh or acquire some other company. "Buy now, pay later," does make sense under certain circumstances. But sooner or later, you know it's going to catch up with you. Either you pay or somebody else will have to pay one way or another.

A rich country that's fighting a war doesn't mind borrowing money or spending whatever it takes to win that war. Victory is all-important. When there's a depression, a rich country doesn't mind going into hock for a while to prime the pump and get the economy moving again. Time enough to get the boat on the desired course when the storm is over.

Wars and depressions are extraordinary circumstances, however. They are emergencies. The United States hasn't been in a real war or a real depression for years, yet we owe all this money and the debt keeps getting bigger and bigger without any real emergency for us to use as an excuse. Every year now, even though there's been peace and a slowly growing economy, the government adds 250 or 300 billion to the national debt, simply by spending that much more than it takes in. And there's no end in sight to that, even though we don't even have a Cold War to blame any more. If we can't make ends meet when there's no emergency, Lord help us when there is one.

Military spending is still the government's biggest expense, but before long it won't be. Congress can always decide not to buy something extravagant such as the B2 Bomber and thereby save us 155 billion or so. And there are other ways the Armed Services can pare back to save money in a pinch. But the second-biggest and fastest-rising expense, which by the turn of the millennium will be number one, is one which the federal government has to pay whether it wants to or not. That's the interest on the aforementioned national debt.

We are currently paying 175 billion dollars a year to service that three-trillion-dollar debt. That's 175 thousand million dollars that is buying us diddley squat. As former Senator William Proxmire pointed out recently, it is an expense that "doesn't educate a single child, build a house for a single homeless family, provide medical assistance to save one human life, or a dime's worth of environmental protection or national defense." It's completely useless. Yet the only way to avoid paying interest on borrowed money is not to borrow the money.

Just because we owe a lot of money doesn't mean we're not rich. But just because we're rich doesn't mean we're not being foolish and thoughtless. We wanted to leave something for our children and grandchildren. Well, we're doing that all right!

Factoids

If you want to convince somebody that you are right about something, it always helps to have the facts to back up your argument. Everybody knows what facts are. Facts are indisputable statements expressing reality. Facts are the stuff that all news stories are theoretically made of. Facts are what we journalists are often told we should stick to. We all have great reverence for facts. Facts, however, are in short supply and are difficult to come by.

Unfortunately, not all of the so-called "facts" we are presented with are, in fact, factual. What we often get in place of facts are factoids. A factoid is a statement that sounds like a fact, walks and talks like a fact, but is, in fact, not a fact.

Factoids frequently have numbers in them. My first experience with factoids came when I was a kid. My mother, instead of telling us not to run through the living room, would say: "Do you realize that 5,268 children dashed their brains out last year on the edges of coffee tables?" A factoid does not meet the test of indisputability, but it *sounds* objective because of the statistics.

Another time, I remember distinctly, I was sipping from an ice-cream soda glass that still had the spoon in it. My mother pointed out that there had been a 15 percent increase in kids poking their eyes out with spoons while drinking from soda glasses. Maybe she got this information from some dependable source, but I doubt it. I suspect, even to this day, that she made it up. Made-up statistics lend a certain weight to an argument.

Journalists do not have to make up statistical factoids. Sometimes the factoid is provided by a government agency or interested party of some sort. Police crime statistics and public Pentagon estimates of enemy defense spending are good examples of pseudostatistical factoidism.

Sometimes people complain that they may be getting facts, but not the "true" facts. A "true fact" is one which supports your own point of view, whatever that point of view happens to be. The converse of this is that there are facts that are "false." They may be accurate enough, but they are not to be trusted because they lead to the "wrong" conclusion. It is like the difference between what happens and what "really" happens.

Any sports official is familiar with this phenomenon. You make a close call and people boo if you call it against the home team. It happens every time. Everybody in the ballpark witnessed the same play. But when the fellow in the striped shirt calls the home team out of bounds, the fans want to kill him. In some countries, they sometimes *do* kill him. Although the ref may have been right on top of the play and could see quite clearly what happened, he failed to notice what "really" happened. When you are rooting for one side or another, you know for sure that what you think you saw was not merely a fact, but a *"true"* fact.

> *What you saw with your own two eyes*
> *They'll tell you is a pack of lies.*
> *For disagreement there is room*
> *About who did just what to whom.*

Ignorance

———

One of the major fringe benefits of working as a news broadcaster is that you get to learn a little something almost every day. Not much, mind you. But a little. In the course of reporting a news story, whatever the subject, you are bound to pick up at least one or two scraps of knowledge that you didn't have before. This is gratifying, but it does not entitle you to feel or act like a know-it-all. Far from it. In fact, the more we find out about anything, the more impressed (or depressed) we are by how little we know.

Perhaps even more impressive (or depressive) is how little the so-called "experts" know. Granted, they know more than we do, but what Thomas Edison said is still true: "We don't know a hundredth of one percent about anything." Yet we always live under the illusion that technology has gone just about as far as it can go.

In 1898, the head of the U.S. Patent Office wrote a letter to President McKinley urging that the Patent Office be shut down permanently since, as he put it, "Everything that can be invented has already been invented." A couple of years ago, Ronald Duncan and Miranda Weston-Smith compiled an *Encyclopaedia of Ignorance:* 443 pages exploring some of that vast land of Terra Incognita. Here is a partial list of the things the experts don't know:

Astronomers don't know the size, shape, or origin of the

universe. They don't know if there's anybody out there. Never mind intelligent life. They don't know whether there's any life at all, except for right here. They also don't know whether any stars other than our sun have planets. Their ignorance is, any of them will tell you, astronomical.

Economists, as a group, are not as humble as astronomers. But no two economists seem to agree on anything. If there is one economist out there who is right, it follows that all the other economists must therefore be wrong. So far in the history of economics, any economist who has been proved right in the short run has always turned out to be wrong in the long run. Any economist with a half-baked theory will find adherents, since all economic theory is half baked.

Medicine has made enormous strides, we are told. But for all the money and effort that has been spent, we still don't know what causes cancer or how to cure it. We keep hearing about breakthroughs in arthritis, but when you get arthritis, they still tell you aspirin is about the best treatment they've got for it.

About half the scientists who've studied the subject will tell you that the earth's atmosphere is heating up. The other half insist it is cooling off. We still don't know what killed off the dinosaurs.

If the past is clouded, the future is more so. Niels Bohr, the Danish scientist, once said, "Forecasting is difficult, especially when it's about the future." Futurists argue about how things will turn out tomorrow, and where we're headed. Is it any wonder? Historians can't agree about what happened yesterday, and how we got where we are now. James T. McSheehy, that most quotable of politicians, once said: "As I look down the invisible pathway of the future, I can see clearly before me the footprint of the hand of fate."

They don't make 'em like old McSheehy any more.

III

CURRENT AFFAIRS

Wet Towels

Do you leave wet towels lying around on the bathroom floor?
I confess I do. It is one of those things I have always felt
sort of guilty about. Only a little bit, mind you, but guilty
nevertheless. A certain amount of water always drips on the
tile floor, and when I've finished toweling off, the towel
drops to my feet. And there, I'm afraid, it stays.

My wife, Jean, never says anything to me about the wet
towels on the floor, but that is something I can understand.
Perhaps I would feel more guilty were it not for the fact that
she sometimes leaves her wet towels there on the bathroom
floor herself.

Since we are the only ones who see these soggy towels,
the outside world need never know of this character failure
of ours. (Jean will be so pleased to know that I have told
you all about it in this piece.) If we were giving friends and
neighbors a guided tour of the bedroom and bathroom, we
would not leave the towels there on the bathroom floor, I'm
sure. But this is something that hardly ever comes up.

Whenever the Osgood children leave their towels on the
bathroom floor, which is all the time, they get a parental
lecture. Never are they to hang those wet towels up (heavy
irony!) there on the bathroom floor again. Hypocrite that I
am, I have pointed out to them that civilized people either
hang towels on the towel rack or put them in the hamper.

Indeed, I was pretty sure this was the case. Hanging towels up or putting them in the hamper is not such a terrible chore. A person who is brought up right should be able to do that instead of leaving them in a soggy heap on the tile floor. The lecture on towel hanging is delivered not as an exercise in hypocrisy, but as part of an overall effort to bring the kids up "right."

But you know who leaves soggy towels crumpled on the bathroom floor? George and Barbara Bush, that's who. The President and First Lady of the United States.

The reason I know this is that Mr. Bush recently did something Ronald Reagan never did in the entire eight years he was President. Bush, exercising his prerogative as Chief Executive to show people any part of the White House he wishes, invited a group of Republican senators and congressmen and their wives attending a White House reception to come upstairs with him to the rooms where the First Family lives. Bush personally led them on a little tour. He sat one couple at a time down on the bed in the Lincoln bedroom and took a Polaroid picture of them, duly signed by the President himself. He showed them his study. He showed them his dressing room. He even escorted the congressmen and spouses into the bathroom. On the sink were Barbara Bush's eyeglasses and some face powder.

And on the floor were (gasp!) crumpled wet towels! More than one! Since the private presidential bathroom is used by no one other than the President and his lady, there could be only one conclusion. Well brought up as they are, the Bushes, like the Osgoods, do leave bath towels on the floor.

I can't tell you how gratified and delighted I was to learn this. Apparently my lifelong assumption that good, clean, decent civilized people would never stoop so low as to throw a used towel on the bathroom floor was mistaken.

Relax, kids, it's okay after all.

Public Service, Private Lives

I hope no President ever nominates me for any high public office. I'm pretty safe there, since it's unlikely any President ever would. But for your sake, I hope no President ever nominates you, either. Don't get me wrong. You'd be great, I'm sure. It's just that being nominated for high office such as Supreme Court Justice or Secretary of Defense is one of the worst things that can happen to a person in this country.

You can be doing just fine, somebody in the prime of life with distinguished achievements, making good money, having an outstanding career with self-respect and the respect of family, friends, and the world at large. And then suddenly this terrible thing happens to you. It's like being struck by lightning or run over by a truck. The President of the United States calls you up one day and says he wants you to be a Supreme Court Justice or Secretary of Defense.

Oh, no! Please! Not that! Anything but that! Aaaaargh!

Until that moment, you could take for granted a reasonable amount of privacy in your life. You could hold your head high and go through a whole day sometimes without people saying mean, disgusting, and insulting things about you, either to your face or behind your back. You could pick up a newspaper or turn on the radio or television without encountering some vague, unsubstantiated speculation about your drinking or sexual habits. But once you are a nominee, it's like deciding to run for President. You become a second-class citizen, the butt of jokes, the target of character assassins.

In the United States we try to bend over backwards to protect the rights of accused murderers, thieves, child molesters. But the solicitude we show to those accused but not yet convicted of high crimes is denied to those nominated but not yet confirmed to high office.

It is the Senate's job to approve or disapprove of a President's choice for a cabinet job. It's proper and fitting that a person's qualifications and experience be looked into. In the case of John Tower, it was fair to inquire about his connections with defense contractors and where his loyalties lay. If you can't stand that sort of heat, you stay out of that sort of kitchen.

But when overheard restaurant conversations get printed in the papers, when anonymous accusers in silhouette with their voices electronically masked go on national television to talk about secretaries being chased around desks, when every day there is page-one speculation about drinking and womanizing, it certainly does give a clear field to anyone who wants to do mischief and destroy a person for political reasons, doesn't it?

Why would any sensible person subject himself to this sort of pain and public humiliation? Is it any wonder that it is getting more and more difficult to get the most able people we have in this country's private sector to go into public service at the highest levels? Anybody who enjoys that much abuse must be crazy, and we certainly don't want a crazy person to have that much power!

And while we're at it, if a man runs for President and loses, how long does he and his family remain public property? Why, if Kitty Dukakis checks into a rehabilitation clinic to deal with a drinking problem, is it any of your business or mine? If her husband had won the election and she were First Lady, that would be another thing. But she is not. She is not even up for Secretary of Defense!

Have a nice day, and if President Bush calls, tell him I'm not home.

National Secrets

———————

You can see why national security might be a consideration in the Oliver North trial. The good colonel was, after all, working in the White House, although apparently nobody else in the building realized what he was up to. Nor were they supposed to. It was a secret. North's duties involved many secrets. Not just ordinary secrets that ordinary people might whisper into each others' ears. I'm talking *national* secrets, the kind only very special colonels and FBI and CIA agents whisper into each others' ears. You would not want these secrets falling into the hands of the Russians, because if the Russians found out they might tell some member of Congress. Members of Congress are the *last* people you want to find out about national secrets. Everybody knows that.

I guess the Secret Service must have some secrets, too, otherwise it wouldn't be known as the Secret Service. You can usually spot a Secret Service agent because he wears a little plastic earphone in his ear, sort of like a television anchorman. This little earphone enables the Secret Service man's superiors to whisper national secrets into his ear at a distance. Never mind what secrets. That is none of your beeswax, if you don't mind my saying so.

So far at the North trial, the main thing everybody has worried about is making sure that no national beans get spilled, that no national cats get let out of the bag, so to speak. If something comes up at the trial that touches on a national secret, it might make its way into a newspaper, and a foreign intelligence agent might happen to read that newspaper, and then next thing you know the secret is compromised. The Russians and the Chinese will find out about it, not to mention the Libyans and the Iranians. After that it is only a matter of time before Congress catches on.

A federal judge in Newark, New Jersey, has recently dealt with a fascinating national secrets case. It seems that six years ago, when Todd Patterson was eleven years old, he decided to put together his own "world encyclopedia." So he wrote to 169 countries asking for information. He wrote the letters on the letterhead of his father's company, Laboratory Disposable Products.

The FBI apparently notices when mail comes in from certain countries, and Todd's parents noticed that some of the mail, especially from the Soviet Union and places like that, looked as if somebody had already thumbed through it. Actually, it looked as if somebody had sat on it, stepped on it, and run over it with a bulldozer.

When they found out the FBI had a file on their kid, who is now seventeen, the Pattersons sued the FBI. They wanted a thousand dollars damages for each incident of intercepted mail, etc. And they wanted to see the whole file on Todd. The Bureau said no, they couldn't do that without spilling some national beans and letting some national cats out of the bag. Judge Alfred M. Wolin has ruled that the FBI acted lawfully, did not violate the boy's privacy or First Amendment rights. Judge Wolin also decided that he can't order the Bureau to turn its file on Todd over to Todd and his parents because it might jeopardize national security and compromise national secrets.

Does the FBI have people on duty at the Post Office checking to see what mail comes in from where and whom it's addressed to? Don't know. That would be a national secret, I suppose. The sort of thing that would be highly dangerous if Congress ever found out.

The Fair Weather Helicopter

The folks at the McDonnell Douglas Helicopter Company must be sick and tired of having people laugh at their Apache Helicopter. After all, the Apache is not a joke. It is the U.S. Army's top line–attack helicopter and the Army has already bought 675 of them, and plans to buy 132 more this year, for a total of 807 Apaches at a cost of 12 billion dollars. Serious money.

So you have to promise not to laugh when I tell you that the hi-tech all-weather choppers failed to function properly during the early hours of the Panama invasion in December 1989. Why? Because it was raining. Pilots had difficulty flying the Apache through the rain because the raindrops and humidity caused moisture to build up on the hi-tech electronic components. Mechanics had to use heaters to dry out the parts before they would work right. I am not making this up, I swear.

An all weather–attack helicopter that doesn't work too well when it's raining is not much of an all weather–attack helicopter, some cynics might say. If it had been hail, or snow, or fog, or gloom of night, who knows, maybe everything would have been all right. But rain, apparently, was something they weren't ready for.

The Apache is quite wonderful, the Pentagon explains.
It works in any weather, unless of course it rains.

Twelve billion dollars isn't such an awful price to pay
Let's hope that when we need it, it will be a sunny day!

This is the last straw as far as investigators for the General Accounting Office are concerned. It was bad enough that the Apache was a "maintenance nightmare" as the *Arizona Republic* called it. It was bad enough that the Apache's guns tended to jam and the main rotor blades would sometimes fall apart. It was bad enough that the bearings in the Apache's tail rotor were inclined to overheat. But having to blow-dry the Apache every time it rained was just too much! Stop laughing like that!

The GAO will be issuing a full report later. In the meantime, however, word is they're recommending that Congress put its foot down and not let the army buy the additional 132 Apaches budgeted for this year. It looks as if the 1.49 billion dollars may be needed just to maintain the ones they've already got.

Right from the start the Apaches have been a headache. The first several hundred did so poorly in field exercises that Army Colonel R. Dennis Kerr complained. The helicopters did everything they were supposed to do only 49 percent of the time. That's not so good, nor what you'd call terrific reliability.

The hope was that performance would improve as the choppers were broken in and the kinks worked out. But instead, as the Apaches' flight hours increased, their ability to perform decreased. In other words, the more you fly one the worse it gets.

Still, it isn't very nice of people to laugh. If there is any joke, it's on the taxpayers.

Who Put the Plastique in Mrs. Murphy's Baggage?

Used to be, when you checked your luggage aboard an airline flight, the principal worry you had was that you would land in Chilacothe and your suitcase would be sent to Kalamazoo. The only other thing you were concerned about was that somebody might open one of your bags and take something out. Nowadays, what you want to guard against is the possibility of somebody opening up one of your bags and putting something *in*. Something that might explode.

Reinforcing that anxiety are the questions airport security people ask you. "Did you do all the packing yourself or did somebody do it for you?" "Are you carrying any packages for anybody else?" "Did you leave your bags unattended at the airport or anywhere else, even for a few minutes?"

Even if they don't use the "B" word, it's clear that the one thing they want to be sure of is that somebody didn't plant something that goes bang in your baggage. It's a decidedly unpleasant thought, but one that has been thrust upon us by harsh experience.

In April 1990, somebody put some plastique explosives, a half-pound package of a putty-like substance called C4, in a suitcase that had just been unloaded after an Eastern Airlines flight landed at Milwaukee. It had not been in the luggage while the plane was en route, only afterwards, when Milwaukee Sheriff's Department deputies put it there to test the proficiency of dogs trained to sniff out drugs or explosives. This time it wasn't a terrorist who put the plastique in the suitcase; it was the authorities themselves.

The dog passed the test with flying collars, barking and pawing at this one particular suitcase where the explosive had been planted. "Good dog, Rover, atta boy!!" The handlers were so pleased with the dog's performance that they forgot to take the plastique *out* of the suitcase when the exercise was over. It wasn't until several days later that the plastique turned up missing, and the Sheriff's office figured out the explosive package must have been left in the passenger's suitcase. Oops!

The owner apparently got off the flight, claimed the bag, and was gone with it before any of the sheriff's men remembered to unplant the planted plastique. This was not as bad as it sounds, since there was no way the explosive could explode, without a blasting cap or detonator. It wasn't going to go off all by itself in somebody's car trunk or hall closet. Still, the deputies would feel a lot better about it if the plastique could be found and recovered.

They started going over the passenger manifests of the Eastern flight and any other flights that arrived around the same time that day. They called around asking if by any chance anybody had found a surprise package with their clothes when they unpacked.

Lieutenant John Lagowski of the Milwaukee County Sheriff's Department explained to reporters that there was no violation of policy involved in slipping some explosives into an unsuspecting passenger's suitcase. That was all quite routine. Yes, indeed. Happens every day, he said, at airports across the country. The airlines and the FAA know all about it and don't mind a bit. The only lapse was forgetting to take the stuff out when the sniffing exercise was over. It is important to remember to do that.

It may not have occurred to you that law-enforcement officers might from time to time stuff explosives into your two-suiter. Now you know.

The Mysterious Tunnel

Every man-made thing eventually becomes a ruin. Buildings and bridges, statues and monuments all crumble. It's only a question of time, no matter what they're made of, no matter how well they're constructed. A few centuries later they are all rubble.

Ordinarily we can figure out from the shape of a thing what a given ruin used to be. This was a temple. That was a theater, a stadium, a racetrack, or whatever. But not always. Stonehenge, that circular array of prehistoric megaliths on Salisbury Plain in England, had us baffled for centuries. We're now told it was probably an astronomical observatory of some sort three thousand or so years ago. That's an educated guess, but it's a guess all the same.

The other night one of our own modern astronomical observatories suddenly became a ruin much sooner than anybody expected. The three-hundred-foot dish that was the heart of the giant telescope at the National Radio Astronomy Observatory at Green Bank, West Virginia, just collapsed of its own weight. After a mere twenty-six years, the blink of an eye in astronomic reckoning, the supports holding the thing up gave way and down it came. Like Humpty Dumpty, as one shocked astronomer put it. Mapping the universe is going to have to wait now until they rebuild the radiotelescope on the site or build another one somewhere else.

If the present wreckage simply stays there as a ruin,

someday a future civilization might find it and wonder what in the world it was. Some kind of religious symbol? A device for collecting prodigious amounts of rainwater? Unless we leave them a pretty good indication of what it was, they might have trouble figuring it out for themselves. Even if the Green Bank dish hadn't collapsed Tuesday night, it was bound to fall sometime, sooner or later. It just turned out to be sooner, that's all.

The folks in Waxahatchie, Texas, are unlikely now to think of their pet project as a ruin. They can hardly wait for the new superconducting supercollider that's supposed to be installed in those parts. If Congress comes through with the money, the Department of Energy is planning to dig an underground tunnel shaped like a doughnut, a big doughnut fifty-three miles around.

Atomic physicists say they have to have this, even though it's going to cost 4 billion dollars-plus to build, so that they can pump the air out of it to make a vacuum, then cool the tunnel to minus 452°F, and use ten thousand special magnets to whip protons around in there faster and faster until they crash into each other at nearly the speed of light. If that's what they say they need, who are we to argue? Aside from the fact that we're the ones who'll be paying for it, of course.

At any rate, when the superconducting supercollider becomes a ruin, as one day it must, imagine how much fun everybody will have trying to figure that one out! The tunnel will look *straight* to those who first find it. And then fifty-three miles ahead they'll find themselves right back where they started from. They are sure to wonder what kind of people would build a great mysterious tunnel to nowhere.

For some reason we never think, when we're building something new, shiny, and wonderful, how it's going to look as a ruin. Any more than we imagine our sporty new car rusting in the junkyard. At least with cars you can tell what they used to be once upon a time. With superconducting supercolliders, it's tough.

Keeping Up With the Nakemuras

I don't know about you, but I'm getting just the least little bit fed up with being told that I should be more like the Japanese. Not that the Japanese aren't fine people with splendid qualities worth emulating. It's just that I don't want to be more Japanese than I am. Maybe it's un-American these days not to want to be more Japanese, but I can't help it. So sue me. Or Susumi, as they say in Yokahama.

The latest outfit to compare you and me unfavorably with the Japanese is the American Business Conference. This group of public- and private-spirited citizens has been studying our spending and saving habits and has come to the conclusion that you and I are spending money like drunken sailors. We walk past a store display window, spot something we like, and immediately reach for the old credit card. We Americans, if I read last week's Conference report correctly, can resist anything but temptation.

It wouldn't be so bad if we saved our money to splurge now and again. But we splurge without having saved up. That's our problem, they say. The Japanese aren't like that. They love to save money. While we go out and squander the money we don't have yet on the cars and TVs and VCRs and cameras they make, they save a bundle by not spending a nickel, or whatever the yen equivalent of a nickel is, on anything we Americans make over here. No wonder our balance of payments is out of whack.

According to the American Business Conference, it would be good for the American economy if you and I spent less and saved more. Admittedly, economics is a dismal science, and hard to figure out sometimes, but wouldn't you think it would be good for business for us to go out and buy things? Especially if we could see our way clear to buying some American things?

The frugal Japanese aren't buying American-manufactured products, but they are investing in American property, American companies, and U.S. government securities. You and I may not have U.S. Treasury Bonds salted away somewhere, but that's because we're not keeping up with the Nakemuras, savings-wise. One way we could be more Japanese, they say, is to invest in America the way the Japanese do.

The Conference report says we've been worrying too much about our Uncle Sam's budget and not enough about our own. This is a song that will be music to the ears of many politicians in Washington, who deep down don't like to see you and me spending our money, because they don't think it really belongs to us. They think it belongs to them, and that they're the ones who should be spending it.

The report proposes a new kind of U.S. government bond, a "super saver" bond that would pay premium high-interest rates and would mature in only seven years. That might encourage us to save more, or that's the hope anyway. The last time Washington decided to encourage us individuals to save, you'll recall, was when they came up with the Individual Retirement Account. You and I were going to be able to put away enough, tax-free, so that we could retire with a nice little nest egg, remember? And then they decided the heck with that and they changed the rules on us.

Very tricky, these Americans.

Good Old American "No-Can-Do"

Once upon a time we Americans had an amazing amount of confidence in ourselves. If there was a challenge, a job to be done, we may not have known *how* we were going to do it exactly, but there was no question in our minds we'd find a way. This was the famous American "can-do" spirit. And sure enough, most of the time we pulled it off. I can remember reading signs on shop windows:

> "THE DIFFICULT WE DO IMMEDIATELY.
> THE IMPOSSIBLE TAKES A LITTLE LONGER."
> —THE MANAGEMENT

That was us, all right. Brash, bold, unrealistic, and unsophisticated. But also, by the way, the wonder of the world. Now, of course, we're a lot more analytical. American management is a whole lot more sophisticated and scientific now than in the old days. One of the things we're much better at today is realizing all the things we can't do. Today the sign would have to read:

> "NOTHING IS EASY ANYMORE,
> AND THE DIFFICULT THINGS ARE IMPOSSIBLE."
> —THE MANAGEMENT

For example, there is a billion-dollar piece of business out there waiting for somebody to get. Some company is going to make a bundle manufacturing the tubes for the high-resolution display screens the Federal Aviation Administration is buying as part of a three-billion-dollar update of the air-traffic control system. So far two companies have bid on the job. Both of them are Japanese.

No American corporation is ready, willing, or able to make the commitment to deliver the tubes when the FAA says it wants them. Chicago-based Zenith says it might be willing to make a bid if the agency would hold off a year or so, and if the government or somebody would also kick in twenty or so million dollars for some additional research.

The biggest technological race going on in the world right now is related to this question of high-resolution video tubes. The Pentagon is offering thirty million dollars in seed money to private industry to work on High Definition Television (HDTV), because of its many military applications. But Zenith's boss, Jerry Pearlman, says that money will only scratch the surface. A hundred million a year for four or five years would be more like it, he thinks.

HDTV may very well revolutionize the entire television industry in years to come, some experts believe. They say in a couple of decades it could be a 140-billion-dollar business. But of course there is no guarantee of that. Besides, a couple of decades from now is much too far away for modern American management to be thinking about. "In the long run we are all dead," is a saying many American business school graduates love to quote.

The company that gets the FAA contract is going to be given an enormous boost in the worldwide competition for HDTV. Too bad it won't be an American company.

We once used to crow about "get up and go."
Our "can-do" we depended upon.
Let's pray it's not so, but our get up and go
Seems to have got up and gone.

The Enemy

If you are going to compete, it is necessary to have somebody to compete against. In order for one party to win, whether it's a war, an election or a baseball game, there has to be somebody else who loses. There's just no getting away from that. So unless we decide not to compete, there's got to be at least one enemy, or opponent. Usually, more than one.

It took a little while after World War II for some of us to get used to the fact that our old enemies, the Germans, Japanese, and Italians, had become our dear friends, and that our former allies, the Soviets and the Chinese, had become our "enemies." But it was made clear by words and deeds, both theirs and ours, that enemies are what we had become.

Now, of course, in the era of *glasnost* and *perestroika*, the leaders of the Kremlin and the People's Republic no longer seem such implacable foes. And apparently there are things about our way of life that don't seem as decadent to them now as they used to. The Cold War is over and we won. So who is the enemy now? There are bad guys out there, to be sure, and some of them, including Libya's Colonel Khadafy, are obviously not friendly to us. We have assorted thorns in our national side such as Cuba's Castro. But these are not real "competitors" in the sense of being in our own league.

Now the "them" that we hear most about are our former enemies and ostensible friends, the Japanese. The Zeros they are throwing at us now are not warplanes, but the strings of 0000s that define the trade deficit, and the fact that they are beating our pants off. If we won the war, there is little question that the Japanese have been winning the peace. They do not even worry about us as a competitor. When they think of us, it is as a market. We are not so great at selling things any more, but we are still the world's champion at buying things.

There are plenty of reasons why the United States became less competitive with the rest of the world. But one reason, if you ask me, is that we have become so destructively competitive with each other. Corporate management now thinks of its own employees as an enemy. Workers think of their bosses as the enemy. Companies don't respect their own customers, and consumers now take it as given that whenever they buy something, somebody is trying to rip them off.

Donald Kanter, a professor of marketing at Boston University, and research consultant Philip Mirvis, have co-authored a book called *The Cynical Americans—Living and Working in the Age of Discontent and Disillusion*.

Their thesis is that Americans are so preoccupied with the fear of being taken for suckers, that cynicism has become a major national disease. Management seems to assume that workers are to be watched like hawks every minute because deep down where it really counts, they're no good and just waiting for the chance to goof off or get away with something. So the workers, who are treated accordingly, become resentful of the boss and think he's the one trying to take advantage.

Our companies tend to think of the consumer as the enemy, and try not to give him a dime's worth more than he's paying for. And the "consumerism" movement has bred customers who take it for granted that somebody is trying to rip them off. The rules that seem to apply are: #1. Never give a sucker an even break, and, #2. Don't be a sucker. If we keep gunning for each other this way, we're never going to be able to compete successfully with the rest of the world.

Pogo was right.

The Almighty Dollar

Americans used to think it was good to have a strong dollar. "The Almighty Dollar," our currency was often called in the old days. Maybe almighty sounded a bit *too* powerful. It sounded as if we were worshipping the dollar. Americans don't like to seem that materialistic. But just plain *mighty* would have been okay. And a *strong* dollar certainly sounded better to American ears than a *weak* dollar. No politician could have gotten himself elected dogcatcher in this country if he made "Let's weaken the dollar" an important plank in his political platform.

However, now that it is Washington's official policy to go out of our way to weaken the dollar, it is unfashionable to refer to currency in terms of weak and strong at all. Instead, we talk about up and down, high and low. What would have sounded downright un-American before: "The dollar is too strong, let's weaken it," is more acceptable when expressed in the new form: "The dollar is too high, let's lower it." We are not talking about power any more, you see. We're talking about altitude. The dollar is thought of not as a weight lifter, but as a tightrope walker working without a net.

On the theory that people in other countries will buy more of our goods and services if the dollar is down, and that we Americans will not buy so much imported stuff if a low dollar makes imports more expensive, Washington has been trying to force the dollar down. But in fact it's been going every which way but down. Sometimes it's been going sideways, but mainly it's been headed up.

This upward mobility is the last thing the U.S. Treasury Department, or the Central Banks, want to see. But currency traders around the world have been bidding the dollar up, because it looks like a good bet to them. That's what makes markets move one way or another, and it doesn't matter if President Bush, Prime Minister Uno, or anybody else doesn't like it. It doesn't happen to agree with the policies of the government, ours or anybody else's.

There's a theory now in vogue that says things really cost the same everywhere, when measured by an imaginary common currency. Prices would rise and fall, of course, but they would rise and fall everywhere by relatively the same amount. That's the PPP theory (Purchasing Price Parity). The fact that the dollar has been so strong lately, whoops, I mean *up* lately, has made PPP believers out of a lot of people. PPP is simply water finding its own level. You can't keep a good currency down, no matter how you try to do it with governmental monetary policy.

Besides, there are factors other than the value of the dollar that have been affecting our trade balances much more than the upness or downness of the dollar itself at any given time. I'm talking about our ability to turn out American products that people in other countries want to buy. Want, as in desire. Desire, as in demand.

Sol Hurok, the great impresario and manager of concert artists, used to say that if the public doesn't want to attend a performance, "nothing on earth can keep them from staying away." If American goods and services are not selling abroad as much as we'd like them to, maybe it's not the dollar that's responsible, high or low, up or down. Maybe they're staying away from the show because they haven't been hearing such great things about the show.

Your Tired, Your Poor, Your Undocumented Foreigners

The communist-bloc countries are very good places to come from. It's very clear now that about half the people who live in these countries want to come from there and move here where we are. The other half don't want to move. They would rather have Western-style democracy come to them. Lately, it seems this is not altogether out of the question.

It's also clear that, given the chance, at least half of South and Central America would like to move to North America. Not to mention half of Asia, Africa, and assorted other continents. The reasons given are usually political, although one suspects that economic, rather than political, circumstances may be at the heart of it. It is simply not possible to open up all our borders and tell everybody in the world who wants to come here that they can. No place else in the world can afford to do it either, and no place does.

The degree to which America lifts her lamp of welcome depends on which immigration category you fall into. Basically, you have six kinds of people who want to move to the United States. You have:

1. Your tired.
2. Your poor.

3. Your huddled masses yearning to breathe free.
4. The wretched refuse of your teeming shore.
5. Your homeless.
6. Your tempest-tossed.

The U.S. Immigration policy is different for each of these categories. Being tired of living in your own country is no longer considered a valid reason for being admitted for permanent residence in the United States. Even being sick and tired of it won't do. Being poor, which is the real reason a lot of people would like to move here, isn't considered a good enough reason, either. In fact, if you are rich you probably stand a better chance of being let in, since you can afford immigration lawyers, you can support yourself, and you're less likely to wind up on the public dole.

As far as your huddled masses yearning to breathe free are concerned, unless they can prove they are being especially persecuted for some reason, the U.S. authorities will not automatically grant them political asylum. In fact, no matter how much they yearn to breathe free, the more huddled the masses are, the less likely the U.S. is to open the gate.

The United States is not in a position to accept the consequences of other countries' overpopulation problems. If you identify yourself as the wretched refuse of some teeming shore, you do not have a Chinaman's chance of getting in. Actually a Chinaman's chances may be somewhat better than most, right now. If you were a Chinese student lucky enough to have been here when the crackdown came, you are permitted, at least for now, to stay.

In spite of the nice words on the Statue of Liberty, in recent years the United States has not been able to cope with our own homeless situation, let alone absorb the homeless from elsewhere in the world. And being tempest-tossed does not make it any more likely you will be issued a green card.

The other day I mentioned aloud that you don't hear much any more about the Iron Curtain, or about the Golden Door. A young professional, the graduate of a distinguished American university, told me that she knew about the Iron Curtain but had never heard of the Golden Door. I can't say I was too surprised.

Under Threat of Death

The death threat against author Salman Rushdie is much worse than your ordinary garden-variety death threat. Unlike the Ayatollah Khomeini, most people who threaten to kill you do not have millions of followers anxious to cater to your slightest whim. And most issuers of such threats are not in a position to offer millions of dollars in reward money. So if you are Salman Rushdie, you know darn well that this is one you better take seriously.

If you are anybody in public life these days, you have to realize that there could well be some nut out there who could take it into his or her head to do you in. You don't even have to be especially controversial. Poor John Lennon may have had his problems, but the last thing he might have imagined was that at that point in his career some fruitcake would come along and blow him away.

Some time ago, even I had a death threat. It was a garden-variety death threat, to be sure, and a pretty small garden at that. It came in the form of a telephone call. The first time, I was out and somebody took the message. An anonymous caller wanted me to know that he did not appreciate the little verses I was doing on the radio. The message was that if I continued doing radio poems, the caller would see to it that I never wrote another rhyme again.

Then, a few days later, he called back and this time I talked to him, man to nut. It would not be kind of you to wonder which of us was which. I tried to get the call traced, but there was no time. He just wanted me to know that he hated me and everything I stood for, and especially the radio rhymes, and if he ever heard one again, my life would not be worth a plugged nickel. Something to that effect.

It was his tone of voice that scared me. He wasn't yelling and screaming and carrying on. He sounded quite methodical. Crazy, but methodical. So I had to ask myself, did I love doing the little rhymes so much that I would risk getting killed? On the other hand, was I so spineless that I would let a voice on the telephone deter me in any way from doing what I had always done? After all, anything you can say in verse you can also say in straight prose.

Besides, one of my best friends, who is none too impressed with my poetic efforts, told me that if this character did kill me and gave as his reason that he was sick and tired of my stupid poems, there wasn't a jury in the world that would convict him of murder. "It would be justifiable homicide if ever there was such a thing," said my friend.

For a while there it did have a chilling effect. The rhyming thing has to be done with some sense of fun and fooling around. Under the circumstances, I didn't find myself going out of my way to fool around or make anything in my pieces rhyme with anything else. So it was a few weeks before I did it again, and then it was just a little couplet at the end of the piece. Gradually, I worked myself into doing it about as often as I had before. There were no more calls, and I didn't get killed. Getting killed would definitely have taken the whole death threat case out of the "garden-variety" category.

It did teach me a lesson, though. It taught me never to take a death threat lightly—my own or anybody else's.

There once was a writer of rhymes,
Who never thought poems were crimes.
And whose one way of fighting
Was keeping on writing
Though it made him feel creepy sometimes.

A Modest Proposal

People tend to feel very strongly, one way or the other, about the abortion issue, and therefore it is difficult to discuss the subject in a rational way without offending one side or the other, or both. On subjects such as war and peace, survival of the planet, and world hunger, that people don't get so worked up about, they can usually concede that there is more than one defensible position and that the other side means well and has some valid points to make.

Not so with abortion. On that particular topic, all people seem to think that they are absolutely and unconditionally right and that the people who disagree with them are absolutely and unconditionally wrong. Arguments on the subject therefore tend to be rancorous, reflecting both conviction and moral indignation. At the outset then, I humbly beg the reader's pardon if my views on this matter do not perfectly coincide with your own.

In 1729, the brilliant Dean of St. Patrick's in Dublin, Jonathan Swift, penned what he called: "A Modest Proposal for Preventing the Children of Poor People from Being a Burden to Their Parents or the Country, by Fattening and Eating Them." People were shocked and horrified, as you can imagine. Swift didn't mind shocking and horrifying people if it would help him get his point across. He did not, of course, really mean to endorse cannibalism or infanticide.

He was simply pointing out the practical case that could be made for it, and the benefits that would be gained from such a policy.

In the case of abortion, I have noticed that people who argue both for and against all profess a great love and concern for humanity. Nobody endorses the killing of children *after* they are born.

When you stop to think of it, the more experience that parents have with a given offspring, the more informed and rational the choice will be as to whether or not to exercise their abortion rights. An ideal time, it seems to me, would be in the teenage years. Many parents are tempted to kill their teenagers, even now when it is quite illegal in most states and carries extremely heavy penalties.

Furthermore, in making the choice to which a woman is entitled, waiting until after the birth would give her a chance to look at her offspring first before deciding.

I have heard it convincingly argued that no one should have to be a parent who does not want to be. But many people think they want children, only to discover in time that babies are a great responsibility. They do tend to make demands and to interfere sometimes with one's career and other important adult considerations. If parenthood turns out not to be all it was cracked up to be, the parents could always then exercise their abortion option when they run out of patience. At least they can say they had given parenthood the old college try and didn't like it. It simply didn't work out.

An additional benefit of legalizing post-natal and teenage abortion, would be that the children could overhear the extended abortion-rights option being discussed by their parents. This would no doubt encourage youngsters to improve their behavior, to turn down the rock music, and to straighten up their rooms. It's just a thought.

—Yr. obedient servant,
Charles Osgood

What You Can't See

We humans are blessed with wonderfully limited vision. If we could see all the potential threats and dangers that surround us, it would drive us totally bananas. We wouldn't be able to function any more. We'd be afraid to get out of bed in the morning, or to leave the house and face the world.

What if you could see germs, for instance? What if the little airborne disease-causing critters, the bacteria and viruses, were visible to your naked eye? "Here comes a flu virus in a dive-bombing attack at eleven o'clock! Watch out!" "There's a squadron of tuberculosis bacilli across the room and they're headed this way!" It would be terrible. Even if the germs were clearly tagged so you could tell which one causes what, you'd be so busy ducking and weaving and covering up that it would be impossible to carry on a normal conversation with anybody at a party, say, or a business meeting. You'd never go to the theater or a concert or ball game. You'd never give anybody a handshake, much less a kiss.

And what if we were aware of the constant undergound movement of the giant "plates" of rock that extend six to nine miles deep underneath our feet? Here we are walking around on the outer shell of a great spinning ball with a hot liquid center, keeping track of time by light, by the day/night cycle of our planet's spin. Meanwhile, below us, in total darkness, these great shelves are slowly moving, building up tensions that are sure to produce earthquakes along certain fault lines. If we could see what's happening down there we'd think twice about building our cities, our bridges, our highways in some of the places that we do. But who would want to be constantly thinking about such a thing? I suppose that when they finally reopened the Oakland Bay Bridge, a lot of people thought about it every day. Well, we'll cross that bridge when we come to it.

What if we could see the pollution in the air? "Ah, but we can!" you say. Well, you can see some, but not all of it. Some of the carcinogens are tasteless and odorless. We cannot see the greenhouse effect, or see the holes being poked through the ozone layer. We have to take some scientists' word for it that these things are going on.

Would you really want to see what's in the things you eat and drink? I don't think so. And it's not just cheese and sausage I'm talking about. If you could see the insecticides and preservatives in foods these days, you might swear off food forever.

They say that in his last years, the late Howard Hughes had become a bit eccentric, to say the least. He was a recluse who didn't like to go anywhere or see anybody, and who reportedly did whatever business he did by telephone. Most of us non-billionaires could not afford to indulge in Hughes's eccentricities. But who knows? Maybe Hughes was not such a fruitcake after all. Maybe his eyes and ears were better than ours. Maybe his problem was that he could see and hear what was there.

The Ice Lottery

The Cold War was, from the beginning, a figure of speech, and nobody thought that when it ended any actual ice would literally thaw. But that shows you how wrong everybody can be. There is some real melting ice in the news, and the United States and the Soviet Union are both involved.

Way up north in the middle of the Bering Strait, between the Seward Peninsula, which is American, and the Chukotsk Peninsula, which is Soviet, there are two islands. Big Diomede and Little Diomede. Big Diomede, which is Russian, is 2.5 miles from Little Diomede, which is American.

The Soviets who live on Big Diomede are soldiers, several dozen of them. The Americans who live on Little Diomede are Eskimos, 150 of them. No Iron Curtain has ever separated the two Diomedes. Most of the time what separates them is ice. You can walk across. But every year in the springtime the ice melts and moves out. The thaw makes the Soviet soldiers and the American Eskimos happy. You would be thrilled, too, to see the ice start to melt if you'd been through the long dark winters they have up there.

Now, in the spirit of *glasnost*, there are plans for an Alaska–Soviet Ice Classic, an international lottery based on selecting the exact time the Bering Strait ice will melt. Even if all the soldiers and all the Eskimos on the islands participated, there wouldn't be enough prize money to put in your eye. But what they have in mind is much more ambitious than that.

"This will be the first worldwide lottery, a global event," says Dan Sullivan of Lottery Alaska Inc., a company that runs charitable lotteries elsewhere in the state. In the Nenana, Alaska, Ice Classic, people buy two-dollar tickets on which they write the exact day of the month, hour of the day, and minute the ice will break up in the Tanana River. A great tripod is set up on the ice, hooked up to a clock. Whoever comes the closest to the time the ice starts to move gets half the money in the pot. The rest goes to local Nenana charities.

Tickets for the Big and Little Diomede or Alaska–Soviet Ice Classic will cost a dollar, we're told. And they'll probably use a different mechanism for making the guesses and determining the winners. Winners plural, because there would always be one prize given on the Soviet side, and one on the American. The money that's raised will go to the Eskimo Village of Little Diomede, and to the Soviet Foundation for Social Inventions, which will run the Soviet end of the show.

Also benefitting will be Camai, a peace group that has organized performing-arts exchanges, has developed ties between Alaska and eastern Siberia, and was instrumental in opening the border there in the far north. "Camai" is the word for hello in Yupik Eskimo.

So while the Wall is being chipped away in Berlin, and the people of Eastern Europe seem more and more to be moving toward, and in some cases to, the West, there now seems great symbolic value in the annual spring thaw up where the Soviet Union and the United States almost touch.

It should be quite inspiring, especially to whoever wins the money.

The Great Crackpot

To begin with, Communism is dead, dead as a doornail. Now that country after country is turning away from Marxism-Leninism, it has become fashionable to say that Communism was an idealistic notion whose only fault was that it didn't really work so well.

Baloney. Communism, if you ask me, was a crackpot idea from the very beginning. It was a silly, pigheaded, unrealistic, utopian scheme that defied both human nature and common sense. It never had a chance of working.

In fact, even though so many countries have called themselves People's Republics and claimed to follow the teachings of Karl Marx, over all these decades, not a single one ever claimed to have achieved Communism. Nobody even came close. Communism was the pot of gold at the end of the rainbow. But it was a mighty long and rocky rainbow. Nobody ever got to the pot of gold.

Before you could get to the pot of gold, where government would simply "wither away" (that's Marx's phrase, not mine), you had to pass through this inconvenient and uncomfortable little phase called Dictatorship of the Proletariat. What this meant was that somebody not chosen by the people would rule in the people's name and call all the shots. No "People's Republic" ever got past this phase, unfortunately.

During this interim period, until Communism was realized, the Communist Party would control the government and the government would control everything and everybody. It would control what the people did, where they lived, where they worked, where they went, what they wrote and read and said and listened to.

This took ruthless purges, a KGB, an NKVD, tanks, troops, an Iron Curtain and a Berlin Wall, to mention only a few parts of the ugly apparatus.

There was quite a difference between communist theory and practice. In theory it would be: "From each according to his ability; to each according to his need." In practice, the way it worked out, was: "From each and to each according to whether or not he's a Party member." If you weren't a Party member it was "from." If you were a Party member it was "to."

What kept everybody going, for all these seventy-five years or so, was that some day Communism would come, and then everything would be hunksky-dorksky.

"When Communism comes," said Boris to Ivan, "everybody will have the use of an airplane to fly around in."

"Why would I want use of an airplane?" Ivan asked Boris.

"Because then," said Boris, "you would hear that they are selling shoes in Minsk. You would get in your plane, fly to Minsk, buy some shoes, and fly back home!"

Communism never came. Not to the Soviet Union, not to Poland, not to Hungary or Czechoslovakia. They were all dictatorships, pure and simple. Proletariat my eye!

What made the Marxist-Leninist countries dangerous to the rest of the planet was their conviction that this crackpot notion was the wave of the future, and that countries that didn't buy Mr. Marx's wacky bill of goods were only standing in the way of their promised communist fantasyland. "We will bury you," Mr. Khrushchev told us in his typically cheerful way.

Oh yeah?

The More Things Change . . .

Back in the bad old days before *glasnost* and *perestroika*, when the Soviet Union was a monolithic communist society, you didn't hear too much about the hatred between Armenians and Azerbaijanis. But now that the Soviet people are free to express their thoughts and feelings, it turns out some of those thoughts and feelings are not entirely based on friendly comradeship or brotherly love. What they choose to say with their newfound freedom of speech is how much they hate each other. Mikhail Gorbachev has his hands full just trying to keep any Union at all in the Soviet Union, between groups that were at each others' throats long before Lenin. The Communist Party chief in Nakhichevan, on the border with Iran, had to quit because of the turmoil in that area with Azerbaijani Shiite Muslims who want union with Iran.

The Lithuanians don't want any part of Moscow either. Some of them want to secede. In Moldavia the Moldavians, who are mostly Rumanian, would rather be a part of Rumania than a part of the USSR. Meanwhile, in Bulgaria, where the Slavic majority despises the Turkish minority and vice versa, towns and cities have been paralyzed by Slavs who want cultural and religious freedom for themselves, but not for the Turks. The songs they've been singing at the protest rallies go clear back to the Ottoman Empire. These people have been hating the Turks since the fourteenth century.

While the Nakhichevan Popular Front is demanding union with Iran, the Iranians continue to loathe and despise the Iraqis, with whom they have fought such a bloody war over the last couple of decades. The only common sentiment held by Iraqis and Iranians is that both of them hate Israel so much. "The enemy of my enemy is my friend," they say in that part of the world. "And the friend of my enemy is my enemy."

We've all seen what has gone on in Lebanon, where the various factions have turned the Paris of the Middle East, Beirut, into a permanent bombed-out shooting gallery. God help someone like Anglican envoy Terry Waite, who tried to get hostages freed. The worst thing that can happen to you there is to become the President. The life of a President of Lebanon isn't worth a plugged nickel.

In Spain the Basques are still up in arms and the Irish "troubles" still plague the Emerald Isle. Blood grudges still get passed on from generation to generation there, as elsewhere in the world. The Eritrians still hate the Ethiopians. Ethiopia and the Sudan are enemies. Pakistan and India don't get along. The Tamils and Sinhalese are wiping each other out. In Punjab the Sikhs are either killing or being killed.

The Berlin Wall may be coming down, but in many ways the world is the way it was when the Kingston Trio used to sing the Sheldon Harnick song "Merry Little Minuet."

> *The whole world is festering with unhappy souls.*
> *The French hate the Germans, the Germans hate the Poles.*
> *Italians hate the Yugoslavs, South Africans hate the Dutch.*
> *And I don't like anybody very much.*

Christmas Tears

———

The crash of Pan Am Flight 103 would have been a dreadful tragedy no matter when it happened. But the fact that it was only a few days before Christmas made it seem all the worse. Christmas is supposed to be a time for joy, not sorrow. It is supposed to be a time for being with people you love, not for suddenly losing them forever, without even a chance to say goodbye.

There was a mother who eagerly went out to New York's Kennedy Airport Wednesday evening to meet her son. It was his birthday and there was going to be a party for him that night. It was only after she checked the Arrivals board and obeyed the message there to "See Agent," that she was told the awful news. "My baby!" she kept crying. "My baby!"

Reverend Frank Rafter, the airport chaplain, knew no words he could use to console her or the others in such pain. He just held the woman, let her cry on his shoulder. What could he say? What can anyone say?

I remember a Christmas a long time ago when I was a little boy, noticing a grown-up fighting back a tear. It seemed a strange thing to me, quite out of keeping with the spirit of the season. It wasn't, but I was too young to realize that at the time. I asked if there was anything wrong and the grown-up said no; it was just that the lights on the Christmas tree and the star on top were so bright they just bothered her eyes a little, that was all.

That seemed a reasonable enough explanation to a child, since indeed the lights were brightly strung and the tree with all its decorations was such pure magic. To a child, everything seems bigger and brighter than it really is. That goes for people, houses, and Christmas trees. And although children are very observant and perceptive about some things, there are others that they cannot be expected to comprehend. They cannot know, for example, that with the joy of loving comes the pain of loss. The closest I had ever come to knowing about that was when my dog Inky had been hit by a car.

My mother and dad were at the heart of Christmas, of course. That was taken for granted. And my brother and sister were there, and grandparents, aunts, uncles, and cousins. There were wonderful smells coming out of the kitchen and a Yule log burning in the fireplace. Friends and neighbors would drop by, and there would be laughter and happy talk. In my memory some of the men are wearing uniforms. Of course they were! We were right in the middle of World War II! Well not in the *middle* of it actually. The battles that were raging were across one ocean or another. Yet here we were, all of us, gathered around the piano, singing the old carols about peace on earth and good will to men. If that seems incongruous now, it did not seem so then. Not to me anyway.

Many Christmases have come and gone. The little boy I used to be is long since all grown up. We have five children of our own and in this season the house is full of family and friends.

The other night there was a familiar carol on the stereo, and as I stood there looking at the tree and musing on the ghosts of Christmas past, one of the kids came up and asked me why I was looking so sad. Was everything all right?

I gave her a hug and assured her that everything was just fine. It was just those beautiful bright lights on the tree dazzling my eyes a little, that's all.

Mr. Murphy

Murphy's law states that if anything bad could possibly happen, it will happen. That doesn't mean the bad thing will happen every single time or even that it will happen this time. But you can bet that sooner or later, probably at the most unfortunate possible moment, the excremental matter is going to collide with the cooling device.

He was not listed on the manifest, but Mr. Murphy was riding on the *Hindenberg* when it approached Lakehurst, New Jersey. He was aboard the "unsinkable" *Titanic* that fateful night as the great ship raced across the North Atlantic on its maiden voyage. Murphy is so innocent looking, his face so unremarkable and familiar, that nobody noticed him going aboard, or if they did, no one realized who he was.

Murphy was on the space shuttle *Challenger*, too, and the *Exxon Valdez*. And he was in a gun turret on the *USS Iowa*. This is not to say that mistakes weren't made, or that each of these tragedies could not have been avoided. But when you put enough high explosives into a confined space in close proximity with enough human lives, all it takes to spark disaster is a spark.

The inquiry into the *USS Iowa* explosion will show, as all inquiries have always shown over the years, that there was mechanical or human failure of some sort. There must always be a reason for these things, some rational explanation that satisfies our need for an orderly, logical chain of cause and effect. Often we look for villains to blame. Sometimes we find them.

But even so, in a larger sense, Murphy is the villain. Is it possible for a drunkard to be in charge of a supertanker? Apparently it was. But we have set ourselves up for disaster by the way we live. It is simply not possible to run super-tankers across the ocean and up and down the coasts without the possibility of disaster. And where there is the possibility, there is inevitably, the reality. The oil spill in Alaska was not supposed to happen, but it was bound to, sooner or later. Bhopal wasn't supposed to happen either, or Chernobyl. But they did.

Is it possible for a terrorist to put a bomb on an airliner? Apparently it is. We try to make it difficult, but there are so many flights between so many airports all over the world at any given time that there is simply no way to make it totally impossible. Therefore, even with every seat sold, there is always some room for Mr. Murphy.

With the best of intentions, we have devised and man-ufactured all kinds of murderous weapons. In the East and West, there are thousands of missiles waiting at this moment to carry their nuclear warheads on missions of destruction around the world. They are not supposed to go off acciden-tally. All we can say is that they have not so far. They are only supposed to be used in the unlikely event of a nuclear war. But of course, there is never supposed to be a nuclear war, is there?

Mr. Murphy is a very old man with a well-worn passport. He travels freely around the world by all known means of transport. Although he has been through so many catastro-phes, he has survived them all. Others die. Murphy always walks away.

IV

THE PURSUIT OF
HAPPINESS

Happy? Don't Ask! (I)

The Pursuit of Happiness is something to which you and I have an unalienable right, according to the Declaration of Independence. Pursuit of Happiness is right up there with Life and Liberty. But pursuing happiness and actually catching up with it are two completely different matters.

Are you happy? Maybe this is not such a good question to ask. Not too often, anyway. As soon as we start taking our own happiness temperature every five minues, we are in danger of becoming unhappy. Unhappiness starts, they say, with wanting to be happier than you are. Even if you start out being reasonably happy with the way things are in your life, when you start to think about it, you soon get to wondering if you are happy enough.

A nagging sense of inadequate happiness is enough to get anybody depressed. Seldom do you see anybody who is both depressed and happy at the same time. You start looking around to see if other people seem to be happier than you are. If they are, you envy them. Of course, they may be stupid enough to be envying you, but you have no way of knowing this. Envy and happiness don't go together well, either.

One of the things that often gets in the way of happiness is worry about tomorrow. "Cheer up!" people say, "things could be worse." What you're afraid of is that if you do cheer up, things will *get* worse. You're afraid if they do get worse, you will be unhappy then, and the prospect of that makes you unhappy now.

Happy marriages are not those in which the two partners sit around fretting about the degree of happiness being enjoyed. Such discussions invariably lead to speculation as to whose *fault* it is.

Sometimes, when we ask ourselves whether we are happy, we imagine that we *would* be happy if only we could get something or other that we want, or get rid of something that we don't want. If we don't get what we want, then we're unhappy that we didn't get it. If we do get it, there's always the possibility that it will become one of those things we decide we don't want, because it does not bring true happiness and is therefore not as wonderful as we thought. Either way it's a setup for disappointment. So don't make yourself miserable by trying to figure out whether you are happy.

The bumper sticker tells us: Life is Hard and Then You Die.
There's no guarantee of happiness, although it's worth a try.
It's important to be happy, all philosophers agree,
But the less you think about it, then the happier you'll be.

A Whole Lot of Yelling Going On

Apparently it is now considered okay to yell at people. I was brought up to believe that it wasn't nice to raise your voice in anger. Now, instead of feeling guilty about yelling, people seem to yell at each other just to let off steam. They actually feel better after they've yelled at somebody.

Motorists who once settled for a honk of the horn and an obscene gesture or two, now aren't happy unless they pass out a little verbal abuse as well.

It does no good, of course. The yeller seldom gets any satisfaction from the yellee. In fact, the yellee seems more determined than ever to keep on doing whatever it is he's being yelled at about.

This new permissiveness, when it comes to yelling, applies only to strangers, however. You are not supposed to yell at your wife, or your husband. It is considered very poor "parenting" indeed to yell at your kids, and they, conversely, are not supposed to yell at you.

Nor is yelling rewarded in the workplace. In today's offices, bosses seldom actually raise their voice anymore. They know that yelling and screaming are not regarded as acceptable tools of modern management. An icy sneer will do the job just as well.

But out on the street, or in the relative anonymity of traffic, many individuals who have been biting their tongues all day begin yelling like banshees, you may have noticed, using colorful words and phrases that would have made the late Lenny Bruce blush.

Some of us refrain from yelling at other people only because we're afraid they will yell back. Lately, I've heard a fair amount of yelling at inanimate objects. The driver in front of me in New York City the other morning stuck his head out of the car window and started yelling for the traffic light to change. It did change, by the way, but I think it was about to change anyway.

I, myself, have been known to yell at typewriters and power lawnmowers. Like human beings, inanimate objects pay no attention whatsoever when yelled at.

In the eastern Solomon Islands is an island called Ulawa, where for countless generations people have believed they could frighten trees to death by yelling at them. Tradition here has it that a tree too big to be chopped down can be killed by simply creeping up on it very early in the morning and suddenly letting loose with a piercing scream.

The tree doesn't fall right over, they say. You have to keep yelling at it this way every morning for a month.

The local belief is that the tree finally goes into shock from being awakened so violently and so often. Ulawans are sure that this method works and nobody has ever been able to convince them otherwise.

Frankly, I think there might be something to it. My evidence is *not* the island of Ulawa, but the island of Manhattan. Every summer, there is a great deal of yelling and screaming in New York's Central Park. Finally the trees can't take it any more. They blush, and the leaves fall off.

Passing the Blame

We all love to say that an idea that turns out to be a good idea was our idea. When something turns out *not* to have been such a good idea, you can never find the idiot who dreamed it up. This tendency of human nature to crave credit and eschew blame has never been regarded as one of our most admirable qualities. We've all been told from the time we were kids that the fine, noble, honorable thing to do is to be generous in handing out credit to others and forthright in accepting blame when things go wrong. Like most noble, honorable fine things in this world, such behavior is exceedingly rare.

This is why, in an election year, the politicians all point with such pride to the stuff they've done, and view with such alarm the stuff their opponents have done. A tad self-serving to say the least. It is one of the reasons politicians are held in such minimum high regard by the public.

Disagreeable as it may be, however, taking all the credit and handing off all the blame may be good for you, according to the latest scientific thinking. At a recent meeting in Philadelphia of the American Association for the Advancement of Science, psychologist Martin Seligman reported that people who blame themselves for their problems are likely to become depressed when the going gets rough. Those who blame others tend to do better and even live longer.

To prove his point, Dr. Seligman cited a study he did of players in the Baseball Hall of Fame. The players who felt that their own errors or failures on the field had cost their teams games or pennants, did not do nearly as well as those who found somebody else to blame. It does wonders for your confidence if when you drop the ball you can tell the world, and even tell yourself, that it was the fault of the coach or the manager, your teammates, the fans, the sportswriters, or the umpire. Especially the umpire. When was the last time you heard a ballplayer explaining a lost game by saying, "I screwed up."

The prisons are full of people who will tell you that they shouldn't be there. It was somebody else's fault, you see. The cop who caught him shouldn't have been there. His lawyer did a lousy job defending him. The judge didn't like the way he parted his hair. Denny McLain never did make it to the Hall of Fame, but he did make it to prison. He used to serve up quite a fast ball; now he's serving up food in the prison cafeteria.

It isn't very nice to take all the credit and hand off all the blame, but psychologists don't much care what's very nice. They just like to tabulate the facts about the way we behave, and the depressing fact is, according to Dr. Seligman anyway, that it's depressing to admit that we've goofed up. How much more satisfying it is to instantly conclude instead that somebody else goofed up.

Success has many parents, it has been said, and failure is an orphan.

Knowing It All

The older you get, the less you know. When I was a young-ster and didn't know anybody and hadn't done anything or been anywhere, I was quite certain of many things. I could see that the older people, the ones who were in charge of running the world, had obviously botched the job rather badly. My fellow kids and I could point out all sorts of mistakes being made all the time by grown-ups, teachers, preachers, the government, the press, and of course, by par-ents. Any number of kids could write a textbook on what it is their parents are doing wrong. What takes the expertise about parenting out of you in a hurry is having children of your own.

Back then, when I still knew it all, I never worried about my own ignorance. It never occurred to me that I was ig-norant. But now that I've been around the block a few times, the things I'm absolutely sure of are fewer, and the things I know nothing about have proliferated. You might think that a lifetime in journalism, getting to meet and converse with successful and fascinating people, experts, artists, sci-entists, presidents of corporations, universities, and even countries, would make a person feel smart and well informed. Not so.

The other day I got to chat with Russell Baker. Baker acknowledged that he, too, used to know pretty much everything. At the age of thirty-seven, however, while working as a reporter for *The New York Times*, it occurred to him one day that, interesting and impressive as his job was, he had become a different person, and the person he had become didn't like doing the work he'd been doing any more. As my friend and former CBS News colleague Hughes Rudd used to complain several times a week: "This is no job for a grown man!"

It is quite liberating and exhilarating being relieved of the crushing responsibility of knowing it all. We spend a good part of our lives trying desperately to convince ourselves as well as everybody else that we know more than we really do. Once we accept and acknowledge our own ignorance, we can stand in a great library and look at all the tall shelves of great books reaching up to the ceiling, and respect even more the collected wisdom of the ages. At the same time, we can understand that it is also the collected foolishness of the ages. Everybody makes mistakes. No shame in that. No individual man or woman is an expert in all things. And even in one's own area of expertise, the longer you study and specialize, the more you know about less and less. Meanwhile, the less you know about more and more.

The more we know, the more we see how little we know. There is some comfort in the realization that we are all in the same boat. While some of us may know more than others about certain things, it is the thinnest slice of all that is or could be known. In that sense we are all profoundly ignorant.

The fact of my ignorance may be relatively recent news to me, but not to others. They've known about my ignorance all along. I sort of like what the late Sam Levenson used to say: "It's easy to be wise. All you have to do is think of something stupid, and then do exactly the opposite."

Last Name First

People sure do get on a first-name basis with you in a hurry these days. One night last week, I got a phone call at dinnertime from somebody I'd never met or heard of before. He asked if I was Charles Osgood and I said I was, and he then asked, "How are you this evening, Charlie?"

I should have hung up and ended the conversation right then and there. In the first place, people on the telephone who want to know how you are this evening do not really give a fig about the state of your health on that particular evening. They are trying to soften you up so they can sell you something, every time. "How are you this evening?" is a dead giveaway.

But not wanting to hurt anybody's feelings, I said I was fine. Actually, I wasn't fine. I was agitated and annoyed at having my dinner interrupted. But torn between guilt and heartburn, I lied and said I was fine.

"Well, Charlie," said the voice on the phone, "I'm glad to hear that." He then proceeded to go into his spiel about the many advantages of modern low-cost aluminum siding. "You know you'll never have to paint again, and furthermore you'll save bundles on your heating bills. You'd like that, wouldn't you, Chuck?" We'd been talking a half a minute and this tin man was already talking as if he were my lifelong buddy. Except for one thing. My lifelong buddies know I hate being called "Chuck."

"I'm having dinner," I said. "I don't want to talk about aluminum siding."

"Gee, Chuck, I guess I got you at a bad time. When would be the best time to call you back?"

"The best time would be never," I said. "I don't like aluminum siding. I don't like being interrupted at dinnertime. I don't like getting an unsolicited sales pitch on the telephone. And I don't like total strangers calling me by my first name. Good night, sir." And with that I hung up.

Apparently, the sort of person who is going to buy aluminum siding from somebody on the telephone is not going to be offended by being called by his first name or some diminutive thereof. In this age of informality, it is apparently believed in some quarters that the sooner you call somebody by his nickname, the sooner you are likely to sell him some aluminum siding.

Dale Carnegie, in his self-help classic *How to Win Friends and Influence People*, mentions that the sweetest sound to any human being is the sound of his own name. Maybe so. But I think Mr. Carnegie meant last name. (I never met Mr. Carnegie and would not presume to call him Dale.)

A recent study by Charles D. Frame of Emory University and Catherine Goodwin of Georgia State University, concluded that most Americans don't like over-familiarity on the part of retail clerks and bank tellers.

According to Professors Frame and Goodwin (not Chuck and Cathy), "Providers of hotel, banking, restaurant, airline and department store services may be well advised to train employees to either use a last name plus an honorific, or no name at all, just 'Sir' or 'Ma'am.' Our research indicates that in those settings, use of first names is poorly accepted by consumers."

Seems to me you don't have to be Al Einstein to realize that. And as Wally Cronkite used to say: "That's the way it is."

Never Put Off Till Tomorrow
What You Can Put Off Indefinitely

I sat down to write a book today. I realized that I couldn't write a whole book at one sitting, but at least I could get started.

But before I could get started, I had to get up and sharpen some pencils. And before I could sharpen some pencils I had to find some pencils.

"Does anybody know where there are some pencils?" I asked the family. "I'm trying to get my book started and I want to sharpen some pencils first, but I can't find any pencils."

"Why do you need pencils?" my wife wanted to know. "You write on a word processor!"

"Well, that's true," I admitted. "But I need to write the title of the book on my diskette label."

Sombody found me a pencil and I sharpened it, turned on the computer, and sat down to start writing the book. It was then that I noticed that the ribbon on the printer needed changing. So I got up and hunted for a new ribbon cartridge, found one, and tried to put it in. But I couldn't get the new one in until I got the old one *out*, and the doggone thing didn't want to budge.

So I called my friend Phil and asked him what to do, and he told me to look at the manual. After a long search, I found the manual, and sure enough, there were instructions on how to do it. So I did it.

Just as I was sitting down to start writing the book, the phone rang. It was Phil. He wanted me to know that he found his manual and could tell me how to change the ribbon now. I thanked him, hung up, and sat down again to write the book. But the monitor screen was full of fingerprints, so I got a rag and dampened it and wiped off the screen.

Then I sat down to write the book, but as I did so, a powerful thirst overtook me, and I realized the writing would go much better if I was sipping on a beer. So I went down and opened a beer, and while there in the kitchen, I made myself a ham and cheese sandwich. This would not hold up the writing, I reasoned, because I could munch on the sandwich and sip on the beer *while* I was writing. So, armed with the beer and sandwich, I sat down to start writing the book.

"This book ought to have a foreword," I thought to myself. So the first word I put down was "Foreward." That didn't look right, somehow. Was it Foreward, Forward, Forword, or Foreword? I went over to the bookshelf to see if other books had forewords or forwards, or what.

After a while, I went downstairs and was walking out the door when my daughter Kathleen inquired where I was going.

"I'm just going down to the store to buy myself a pack of cigarettes," I said.

"But you don't smoke," she correctly pointed out.

"Don't be insolent to your father," I told her.

Today did not turn out to be such a good day to get started writing a book. Too many interruptions. But tomorrow should be much better. Yes indeed. I'll get started on it first thing in the morning.

Turn Right Where the School Used to Be

Traveling by automobile on the back roads of America, as so many of us do in the summer, you can easily get lost. I don't mean really lost; I mean there will be times when you don't know where you are. There is a subtle difference between being lost and not knowing where you are.

Here is how it happens. You are driving south from Point A to Point B, the sun is shining merrily on the lake, and everybody is in a happy mood. Then your teenage daughter asks an insolent question: "Daddy, aren't we supposed to be driving south?"

"We are driving south," you say. "We are headed for Point B."

"But if we are going south," she asks timidly, knowing perfectly well this is going to cause trouble, "how come the lake is on the left? If we're going south, shouldn't the lake be on the right?"

You are, of course, east of the lake, so indeed, the lake should be on your right if you are en route to Point B. Instead, you are obviously headed north, for Point C. But you waffle: "This road twists and turns," you say. "Maybe the lake will be on our right after a while."

"I don't think so," says your wife, consulting the map. "I think we're headed the wrong way."

Just then, you spot a man riding a bicycle.

"Let's ask him," you suggest. What you mean by that is your wife should ask or one of the kids should ask. None of you wants to ask because you've all learned from bitter experience what happens when you ask anybody for directions.

"Excuse me," you say to the fellow on the bike. "Could you possibly tell me how to get to Point B?"

"Point B?" he chuckles. He whistles, shakes his head, and tells you you're headed the wrong way. You acknowledge your stupidity and he says, "Okay, tell you what to do. Turn around and go back till you get to the old church, then you bear left and keep going straight till you pass the Hopkins' place, then pretty soon, you come to the intersection where the school used to be, turn left there, and then hang a right about a mile before you get to the bridge."

"Thanks a lot," you say politely. So you make your U-turn and head back in the direction from whence you came, which is to say, Point A. After what seems an eternity, you come to an old church. There you bear left, keeping a sharp eye out for the Hopkins' place.

"Will there be a sign or something?" your daughter inquires. "How will you know it's the Hopkins' place?"

"Shut up," you explain. "I'm trying to figure this out." Unfortunately, it is true that you don't know what the Hopkins' place looks like. Nor do you know where the school used to be. Nor is there any way to know when you are a mile from a bridge. So your wife says, "Why don't you stop and ask somebody?"

"Oh no," you say. "I already asked somebody. This time it's your turn!" It is at times like these that the difference between being lost and not knowing where you are gets terribly blurred.

Nap Time

The only people who will tell you that money isn't very important are rich people. You tend not to think about what you have plenty of. Hunger has a way of making a person preoccupied with the subject of food and eating.

Similarly, we people who have to get up at three o'clock in the morning to go to work five days a week, tend to get a tad obsessed with the idea of sleep. Other people may scheme and fantasize about sex, money, or power. We early-morning types find ourselves conspiring constantly to get in a little extra shut-eye.

You finally figure out that this is not the way you're supposed to feel when you go off on vacation and keep more civilized hours. Next thing you know you're feeling human again, after almost forgetting what that is like. Not that I would necessarily want to get *too* used to it, mind you. Most people in my profession can only stand feeling human for a few weeks at a time.

Work and sleep schedules can make a tremendous difference in the way you feel. In many parts of the world, it has long been considered uncivilized to work in the middle of the afternoon. In France, Italy, Spain, Portugal, Mexico, and most of Central and South America, there's no point going shopping between noon and 3:00 P.M. The stores and markets are closed.

Banks, travel agencies, and most business offices are closed, too. If you want to do business in those hours, forget it. Everybody goes home for lunch or to a restaurant or café. And some of them go home, close the shutters to keep out the afternoon sun, and grab themselves a little sack time. Later, at 4:00 or 5:00 P.M., they'll be back on the job and working full tilt. But, as Noël Coward used to sing, only "Mad Dogs and Englishmen go out in the midday sun." He forgot about us Americans. We're out there hustling with the Englishmen and the mad dogs.

Scientists are now telling us that the human body was never designed to operate without some down time in the middle of the day. In the preface to a new book called *Sleep and Alertness: Chronological, Behavioral and Medical Aspects of Napping,* published by Raven Press, Dr. William Dement of Stanford University writes: "It seems nature definitely intended that adults should nap in the middle of the day, perhaps to get out of the midday sun."

This is not such a demented notion. NASA has recently conducted sleep experiments and so have medical schools here and in Europe. And it turns out that if you put somebody in a darkened room and take away clocks and other time references, most adults will sleep twice in a twenty-four-hour period. Once for six or seven hours, and then again several hours later for one or two hours. Nappy time.

When little kids miss their afternoon naps, they get cranky and hard to live with. You may have noticed that big adults are often cranky and hard to live with, too. Have you ever wondered why?

Whatever Happened to Parents?

Remember parents? It used to be that in the lives of most kids there were these two grown-ups, one male, the other female, who were in charge. Whatever they said went. Kids didn't always like it, and they didn't always obey cheerfully, but there was little question about who was boss. These two older people would tell you, among other things, to clean up your room, to do your homework, to walk the dog, to practice the piano, to wash your face, to comb your hair, to brush your teeth, to sit up straight at the table, and not to talk with your mouth full.

Young people would resent this sometimes, feeling that they had better things to do than to have to listen to this same tune all the time. Still, you would talk back to parents at your own risk. They were not only older, they were also bigger. Those days it was assumed that being older and bigger and having more experience with life, parents would be in a better position to judge what their children should be required or allowed to do and what they shouldn't. Somewhere along the line the assumption became exactly the opposite; that young people, being more tuned in to "what's happening," would know more, and therefore be in a better position to judge. The opinions of parents, like their experience, was deemed irrelevant. Parents would resent this, feeling that *they* had better things to do than be put down by their very own kids.

There was a corresponding development in the field of education. Schools, which had been considered places where students went to learn something, became something else instead. Day-care centers maybe? Social-adjustment centers? Whatever it was, it didn't have much to do with learning anything.

The Harvard philosopher Ralph Barton Perry once made note of this evolution in pleading for what he called an "Age Movement."

According to Professor Perry, the institution of school was originally created in order that the young might learn from the old who had, when young, learned from their own elders.

"The idea was," wrote Perry, "that the infant was a vegetable, the small child an animal, the adult a human being, and the aged adult a wise human being with a touch of deity. On this theory the individual learned at each stage from a superior who had something to give."

Then along came so-called progressive education and the process was completely reversed.

"The child being a genius and the adult a fossil, nobody taught anybody anything. The child unfolded in accordance with his own creative impulses and the adult provided the tools and conveniences. Meanwhile, as the child grew to manhood, he gradually fossilized until he became a dodo in his own right."

That's what happened all right. But now there are encouraging signs, with the aging of the baby boomers, that experience is being valued more now than it has for a long time. After all, you can't learn from experience until you get a little of it.

Who knows, maybe parents will make a comeback.

Whatever Happened to
Huckleberry Finn?

Where are the kids? Why aren't they out there running and playing and riding their bicycles? Why don't I see kids climbing trees any more, swinging on tire swings, or racing each other to the corner? Why aren't they falling down and scraping their knees and getting their clothes all torn and sweaty the way they're supposed to? Where are the freckle-faced urchins who used to set up the lemonade stands at the curb, and then drink all the lemonade themselves? Today, poor old Norman Rockwell could set up his canvas and easel and sit there all day before he could find a damn thing to paint. Where are all the laughing, shouting, dirty, tousled-haired, out-of-breath kids with the traces of chocolate ice cream on their faces? Did the Pied Piper come and lead them all away? Are they all away on family vacations or off at summer camp? Or is it as I fear? Are all the kids inside in their air-conditioned TV rooms playing Nintendo?

Is that possible? Are they all in there beep, beeping away at Mario Brothers II or Mike Tyson's Knockout? Are they in there being mesmerized by Rambo or Duck Hunt? Is the only exercise they're getting running in place on the Nintendo Power Pad? Is that why there are no kids outside?

At this time of year in the neighborhood I grew up in there were kids everywhere. If you wanted to play with other kids, all you had to do was step outside. There they were.

Big kids, little kids, boys, girls. Dogs, too. In my memory, anyway, the dogs were always with us kids. Running and playing outdoors seemed like a fine idea to the dogs, too.

We didn't have any equipment to speak of. A ball and a sawed-off broom handle were all you needed to play stick-ball. In the summertime all the fun was outdoors, and staying inside the house did not seem all that tempting. In those days, of course, nobody had air-conditioning. Television was unheard of, let alone video games. Toys "Я" Us had not gone into business yet. Unsophisticated as we were, we did not realize that we were deprived and not having any fun. We went ahead and played baseball on a vacant lot, not realizing that to play baseball it is necessary to have an official field, eighteen players, uniforms, coaches, and an umpire. We chose up sides and played with however many kids we had. Somebody's shirt was usually first base.

I don't remember us even once ever running to my parents complaining that we were bored. Not that it would have done us any good. In those days, child boredom was not very high on the adult priority list. Somehow it never occurred to kids to be bored, or that you needed some kind of plastic TV toy, electronic gadget, or supervised, organized activity to enjoy yourself. We played hide-and-seek, and tag. We played cops and robbers, cowboys and indians. (Today it would have to be cowpersons and Native Americans.) We dove into piles of leaves and rolled around. We made make-believe forts, castles, airplanes, and pirate ships. On rainy days we sang songs and played twenty questions and told each other ghost stories and, scene by scene, the plots of movies.

All this would seem pretty tame, I guess, to kids today. Through television they've seen everything and been every-where. They've had sex education and drug education. In their movies and in their play they want action. So to kids nowadays a backyard with some trees in it does not hold the magical possibilities for them that it did for us. It's just a backyard with some trees.

Osgood's Universal Bad-For-You Scale

———

Smoking cigarettes is bad for you. It says so right on the package. Everybody knows that. Everybody also knows that jaywalking is bad for you and so is riding a motorcycle without a helmet. All these things involve taking certain risks. But what I would like to know, on some sort of unified, intelligible scale, is how bad is it to smoke the cigarette and risk coming down with cancer or heart disease, as compared to crossing in the middle of the street and taking the chance of being hit by a truck?

These are unlike things, and you can't compare apples and pears, I suppose, but it seems to me in this day of computer analysis, we should be able to figure out some way to compare the risks involved in the unlike experiences of everyday life. There are risks involved in everything, after all. When you get into a car, you can reduce the risks somewhat by using the seat belt, but there's no guarantee you won't be killed anyway. Does that mean you should stay out of cars? Of course not.

When you get on an airliner, you know that several bad things could happen. The plane could be hijacked. It could be blown up by a terrorist bomb. The fuselage could suddenly rip open for no good reason at thirty thousand feet, and you and your seat could make a sudden, rapid descent. But you get on the plane anyway, because you know that although these things happen, they do not happen a whole lot, relatively speaking. One chance in a million, two out of a hundred thousand, whatever it is. Somebody should be able to work out the statistical probability of all the bad stuff that could happen when you get on a plane, and assign a number to it.

Would it be a higher number or a lower one than getting into a car without fastening your seat belt, or eating a juicy New York sirloin steak or a hot fudge sundae with whipped cream? How does that compare, in terms of risk, with having sex with a stranger or sharing a needle with an addict? I don't know, but somebody must. Or if they don't, there's got to be some way they could find out. Common sense can take you a long way, but since we're talking about life and death, maybe common sense, also known as the seat of your pants, is not the best possible guide to rely on.

These days, in making investment and budget decisions, corporations rely on sophisticated computer programs that work out the projected risk/benefit ratio. How can we be expected to make rational judgments about what to do and what not to do in our private lives unless we can compare the benefits, if any, with the risks, whatever they are? If it's true that commercial apple juice contains a carcinogen, how bad is it to drink a glass of apple juice compared to drinking a martini? How about a couple of glasses of apple juice compared to a couple of martinis? Some risks you might be willing to take, others you would not. You would not, for example, try to drive home after drinking the martinis.

Which is worse, to be twenty pounds overweight, or to walk through Central Park on a dark, foggy night? Which is worse, to go skydiving or to pick up a hitchhiker on a country road? Which is worse, to hold up a liquor store, or to write a novel that makes some Iman mad at you? Inquiring minds want to know.

Happy? Don't Ask! (II)

In his vaudeville act, the late Ted Lewis used to ask the audience: Is everybody happy?" As a newsman, what I have to wonder is: "Is *anybody* happy?"

Most people you hear on radio and television newscasts are angry about something. The situation is unfair, and they're getting the short end of the stick, to hear them tell it.

A friend who worked hard and long to become an executive is not happy now that he is one. The reason is that everybody who comes into his office wants to complain. Just once he'd like to hear somebody say the job is just what he or she had hoped and more. But everybody seems to want more money, more interesting work, and a bigger office, he says.

You might think after struggling for careers like the ones men have, women in the workplace would be happier now than they used to be. But no. *Working Woman* magazine says more than half the readers polled feel they're poorly managed, aren't made to feel important, and get little feedback.

Some workers, both men and women, get so bored on the job, they bring along reading material to while away the time. Some companies don't even like to see books or newspapers brought into the office for reading on breaks. You might think a paper company would encourage books and newspapers. But no. St. Mary's Paper Co. in Sault Sainte Marie, Ontario, is trying to "instill a new work ethic" in its plant, restricting reading during breaks to company-produced pamphlets. Other reading isn't conducive to the company's interests, management says. The Paperworkers Union is unhappy about that and has filed a grievance. And unhappy employees are boycotting by not reading anything. Lawyers will no doubt get involved in that one.

You'd think lawyers might be happy, since there's so much legal work around, and since it's such a well-paid profession. (Average income is $104,625 per annum.) But no. *The American Bar Association Journal* reports 40 percent of the lawyers surveyed say they don't think they make enough money.

> *Everywhere you look it seems*
> *Everybody always dreams*
> *Of getting what he hasn't got*
> *And somehow being what he's not.*
>
> *Other people, in our eyes,*
> *Always seem the lucky guys.*
> *We're the ones whose lot is meaner*
> *Than over where the grass is greener.*
>
> *Some other house, some other car*
> *Than what you drive, or where you are.*
>
> *We envy other people's faces*
> *Yet before you go trade places*
> *Think, for it's most likely true,*
> *That other people envy you.*

V

THIS OLD HOUSE

Out With the New, In With the Old

A friend of mine told me recently that he wanted to buy a new house. When I asked him what he meant by a new house, he looked at me as if this didn't require explanation. "Buy a new house," he said. "I mean a house that nobody has ever lived in before. What else would I mean?"

My family and I live in an old house. Plenty of people have lived in it before. The house was built in 1858. That makes it 133 years old now. So my idea of a "new" house is not the same as my friend's. To my way of looking at things, an old house is better than a new house. The man who built the house I live in built it to last for a long time. And sure enough it has. Not only that, but its life expectancy even now is probably greater than that of the "new" house my friend is going to buy. That's what progress has done for us. Nobody builds things to last a long time any more, houses included. And sure enough, they don't.

Admittedly, when you have an old house, you have to put up with some of its aches and pains. Pipes do get rusty and electrical insulation wears out in time. Old things take some maintenance, that's true. But in many cases they're worth the trouble.

To me there's nothing sadder or older-looking than

something that was trying to be "modern" or "futuristic" and then couldn't take what even a few years of aging would do to it. Near the National Tennis Center in the borough of Queens are the rusted remnants of the New York World's Fair of 1964. They were shiny and new only twenty-six years ago, and now? Well, they were not meant to last, and so now they look a whole lot older than my house, I can tell you. It doesn't take very long for "new" to turn into "old" if you don't take care of something.

We are told that the "infrastructure" in the United States is fading fast, that our roads, tunnels, bridges, etc., are falling apart faster than we are able to keep them up. We're going to have to spend a lot of money on this now, at a time when the federal government is supposedly trying not to spend a whole lot of money on things.

And the part that's falling apart fastest is not the oldest part, but the Federal Interstate Highway system and the bridges and overpasses connected with it. Some of these things are considered old now because they have passed their twenty-fifth birthday! Give me a break!

In the old days, engineers would try to build a bridge that would withstand ten times its expected load. That's why some of the old ones have held up so well. Today's engineers pride themselves in designs that will just barely hold up what they have to. More efficient, no doubt. But better? I don't know.

What is true for a house or a road or a bridge is not necessarily true for an airplane. Older is not necessarily better when it comes to aircraft, although in some cases you could argue that it is. Many of the airlines are still using jetliners that are pushing the quarter-century mark. The people who designed these planes never thought in their wildest dreams that passengers would still be flying around in these things in the year 1991.

Now that a few of the old birds have started coming apart in mid-flight, aviation safety experts say we're going to have to come up with much better maintenance programs for older aircraft and make sure there are people around who still know how to fix them. Sounds like a good idea to me. But then you know how I am about old stuff.

Zlongazyer . . . Whydoncha?

"Zlongazyer . . . whydoncha?" is a phrase familiar to any hapless homeowner, especially to the proud owner of an ancient house. The old Osgood place was built in the Buchanan administration. From time to time (about once every ten minutes), something gives out and has to be repaired or replaced. That's when you get "Zlongazyer gonna do thus and so, whydoncha do such and such?"

A few months ago after I took a bath one evening, the water drained out of the bathtub a little too slowly to suit me. That's all it takes. Little did I realize the long and excruciatingly expensive chain of events this seemingly minor problem would trigger. The rubber plunger and the drain cleaner didn't help this time. So I called the plumber. Several days passed.

"Zlongazyer gonna hafta fix this drain," said the plumber, "whydoncha fix the other pipes here in the bathroom, too? They're all shot." It had started. The dreaded zlongazyer, whydoncha sequence was underway.

"Zlongazyer gonna hafta fix the old pipes," volunteered Mrs. Osgood, "whydoncha see about redoing the floor and wall tiles? We'll have to dig up some flooring and tiles to put the pipes in anyway." One thing led to another. Several others, in fact.

"Zlongazyer gonna redo the walls and floor," suggested

the bathroom man, "whydoncha put in a whirlpool bath, a new toilet, a bidet, a sauna, and a steam shower?" Last week's whydoncha was today's zlongazyer.

"Zlongazyer gonna be putting in all that stuff," said the contractor, "whydoncha let us draw you up some plans?" Several weeks passed.

"Zlongazyer gonna be modernizing the whole room," said the contractor's nephew, the designer, "whydoncha take down this wall, remove that closet, and extend the bathroom to include the room next door?" The room next door was my office, by the way.

"Zlongazyer gonna be doing that much renovation," said the lady at the bank, "whydoncha forget about a home-improvement loan and apply for a new mortgage?"

"Zlongazyer gonna refinance the house," the contractor proposed, "whydoncha have us do the rest of the second-floor remodeling while we're at it? We'll reopen your bedroom fireplace, remove the bedroom closet, restore the room to its original size, and move Jamie up to the third floor."

"Zlongazyer gonna do that," said the contractor's brother, the carpenter, "whydoncha open up the ceiling in Winston's room, add a window, put in a staircase to a loft, and put his bed up there?" Several months passed.

"Zlongazyer got all the walls opened up like this," said the contractor's cousin, the electrician, "whydoncha pull this old wiring out and get it replaced, and zlongazyer doing that, whydoncha run new telephone lines, too?"

One thing, the zlongazyer, leads inevitably to another, the whydoncha. The whydoncha then becomes a new zlongazyer, and the sequence continues *ad infinitum* and *ad destitutum*.

Fix-It Season

This is the season that brings out the Mr. Fixit in every homeowner. Little jobs like putting up the screens, mending fences, painting the porch, etc., give us every opportunity to show what we can do. Or, in my case, to show what we cannot do.

Year after year, I have proven over and over to myself and everybody else in the family that there is hardly any job around the house, regardless of how small and trivial, that I cannot turn into a major disaster. When they see me coming with a hammer or screwdriver in my hand, they act as if I were Jack Nicholson about to go berserk in *The Shining*.

Hang a picture? Sure. Where do you want it? It's a good-sized picture, but I figure why go all the way to the hardware store just for a picture hanger? I'll just hang the thing on a nail. Bang, bang, bang goes the hammer. Bend, bend, bend goes the nail. Crack, crack, crack goes the plaster. Now there is an ugly, cracked place in the wall but no nail and no picture. So I try again, and this time, although the plaster cracks some more and this nail bends, too, it does, just barely, stay up there in the wall, and I hang the picture on it. A few hours later, in the middle of the night, I wake up to an awful noise. Crasho, bango, tinkle, tinkle, tinkle. Sounds for all the world like a heavy picture frame and some glass shattering into little pieces. Is there any *other* little job you'd like me to take care of?

Stack the firewood in the backyard, you say? No problem. I simply put one layer of logs on top of another, and then another on top of that. What could go wrong? Of course, some of the sticks are oddly shaped, and some are bigger than others, but you just sort of *force* this or that piece where it doesn't seem to want to go, and in no time at all, you have the wood all stacked. Admittedly, it's not the neatest thing you ever saw, but the job is done. Again, in the middle of the night, there is a crash. This time a louder, more terrible sound as if an earthquake had hit a lumber camp.

Set and wind the grandfather clock in the front hall? Duck soup. I don't know whether I wound it too tight or what, but it took three years before anyone was able to unravel the cables, and on the half hour the bells that used to play the Westminster chimes now play a tune I'm sure grandfather never heard in his whole life. The clock also does something I'd never heard any timepiece do before. It strikes 14.

My most memorable achievement so far this season had been the meltdown in the gas barbecue. It seems I failed to make sure there were no "cobwebs in the orifice," as the instruction book instructs, and so instead of cooking the steaks, the grill cooked the control panel. The sight of the dials and timer melting was quite remarkable. Surreal, almost. I half expected Salvador Dali to appear in the backyard and capture the scene on canvas.

I envy these guys who never have to hire anybody to do anything because they can so easily do it themselves. When I undertake a Harry Homemaker project, be it in the field of plumbing, electricity, carpentry, or whatever, there is an excellent chance the professionals will have to rescue me sooner or later. Sooner, probably.

Slope

Either they didn't know how to make floors level in 1858, or the house has done an awful lot of settling these last 133 years. I say this because all the floors seem to have a decided slope to them.

If you drop anything the least bit round, a ball, a marble, an orange, or a coin, let's say, in the front bedroom upstairs, it will roll out of the front bedroom into the front hall, past Grandma's room, down the four steps to the back hall, past the laundry room, and all the way to the back stairway. I know because I have chased such runaway objects on several occasions.

Sometimes they will even roll down the back stairway and into the kitchen all by themselves. You can hear such objects coming for quite a while, as if magically self-propelled. It's sort of frightening at first, like telekinesis out of a poltergeist movie. What is happening is not magic, of course, but simple obedience to the law of gravity.

In an old house, you get used to the idea of stuff rolling or sliding around like that, since it happens all the time. But it can happen in a new structure, too. Just recently, the University of Washington Hospital in Seattle moved into a brand-new building, and it's been reported that things have been going downhill ever since.

Although the new facility cost 37 million dollars to build, the floors have such a slope to them that supply carts, wheelchairs, and IV stands have been known to take off on their own and start careening down the corridors.

Based on my own personal experience with objects rolling away from me at home, I can tell you that such things pick up speed as they go along. If you can catch a toy truck or a table on casters as it's just beginning to go into motion, you can sometimes reach out and grab it before it gets up a head of steam. But as the runaway object accelerates, it becomes increasingly difficult to catch up with and bring it back to where you want it to be. Experience teaches you to store anything with wheels on it against a downhill wall. It's the same principle as pointing your car wheels to the curb when you park your car on a hill.

At last report, the builder of the University of Washington Hospital was trying to figure out whether he could find some way to make the floors more level, or whether the only course is to tighten the wheels so these things won't go bye-bye quite so readily.

There's an amusement park not far from me, with a funhouse that has slanty floors, and slanty walls to go with them. The eye plays tricks on you in those rooms. Everything in there is slanted at the same angle—the furniture, the pictures on the walls, everything. So the visual cues are all synchronized to make you think straight up and straight down are in the usual positions. It all looks perfectly normal. Then when you try to walk across the floor, you slam into a wall as if you had spent the day in a saloon instead of in a nice wholesome amusement park. It's fun to be fooled in a funhouse. That's what you go in there for. Being fooled in a hospital is a different thing altogether.

In a hospital you want to know exactly where up is and where down is and no kidding around. And you want the hospital furniture to sit still. I'd hate to think of one of those wheeled beds or stretchers they use suddenly taking off with an unsuspecting passenger aboard on an unscheduled gurney journey.

Nocturnal Encounters

I am getting to be very good at identifying objects with my bare feet. When you live in a houseful of kids who leave stuff lying around on the floor, no matter how much you yell at them not to leave stuff lying around, and if, from time to time, you leave stuff lying around on the floor yourself, you must be prepared to step on unidentified objects with your bare feet in the dark.

The most common objects left lying around are articles of clothing. These ordinarily present no problems. When you step on a sock or a shirt, you know right away that you have encountered something other than the floor or the rug, but it is soft and non-threatening. Sometimes you can make out the shape of the shirt buttons, which is your clue that what you have there is a shirt. If you are really good, you can even pick up the shirt with your toes without having to bend down.

Other bulkier articles of clothing can be more difficult to deal with. A shoe, or a belt, for example. Right away you can tell a shoe, because your foot has learned to recognize a shoe when it feels one. Furthermore, you recognize the shape and sound of a shoe as you trip over it. A belt you know because of the odd sensation of a cold metal buckle between your toes.

If, like me, you sometimes read before falling off to

sleep at night, the first thing your feet are likely to touch when you get out of bed is a book or magazine. No problem if it's a magazine. However, if it's a book, especially a thick hardcover book, one corner of the hard cover will get you right in the instep. Seldom can a book make as dramatic an impact on your head as it makes on your bare foot under these circumstances.

If your bare feet hit something cold and clammy in the middle of the night, your body quickly sends a message to your brain that something distinctly unpleasant has happened. This is not necessarily the case. A while back the kids used to play with a substance with the charming trade name of Slime. It was very cold, clammy, and slimy indeed, but aside from the momentary bad feeling, no harm was done. The instinctive horror, I believe, dates back to the years we used to give the dog full run of the house. Some barefoot encounters no doubt helped us to decide not to give the dog free run of the house any more.

My friend Paul Dickson, the writer, recently told me that his worst nocturnal barefoot encounters have been with toys.

Some toys are okay to step on. The only thing I mind about stepping on a teddy bear is that for one awful moment you think you have stepped on the cat. But certain toys seem fiendishly designed to cause as much pain as possible when stepped on barefooted. Jacks, for example. The jack, with its points and spokes, looks like something concocted in the Inquisition for the soles of heretics' feet.

Getting Organized

"One of these days I'm going to get myself organized." I've been telling myself that for years, but this time I really mean it. Today there is no good excuse for not being organized. There is no earthly reason why I should go on the way I have for all these years, writing myself notes on little scraps of paper, and then shoving the paper into some pocket or other, only to have the piece of paper dry-cleaned later along with the suit.

This is definitely not such a good system. Even if the note is not dry-cleaned, it ends up being totally useless. You reach in your pocket and there, along with your wallet, your car keys and assorted junk, is a dog-eared piece of paper with a telephone number written on it. You don't know whose telephone number it is. You don't remember when or why you wrote it down or what it is exactly you are supposed to do. You can't just dial the number and say, "Hi. This is Charles Osgood. I just found this phone number on a scrap of paper in my pocket. Who is this?"

Being disorganized leaves you with the constant feeling that wherever you are, you really should be someplace else, and no matter what you're doing you should really be doing something else.

And I can't go on like this with all this stuff piled up on my desk the way it is. I have an extremely efficient and

capable assistant, but the papers, letters, clippings, magazines, notes, and assorted odds and ends (including a min-
iature bale of cotton somebody sent me from Mississippi)
are not her fault. They are my fault. "Don't worry about
this stuff," I tell her. "I'll take care of it myself as soon as
I get organized." Down in that pile somewhere may be something of crucial importance. I certainly hope not, but it is
entirely possible.

Maybe what I need is one of the special "organizer"
kits they're now selling. How could a person go wrong? They
come divided by time. You can get Day-at-a-Glance, Week-
at-a-Glance, Month-at-a-Glance, even Year-at-a-Glance. You
can get wall organizers, desk organizers, pocket organizers.
They have separate sections for keeping track of invest-
ments, car servicing and repair, bank statements, insurance
policies. They have little slots for coupons, receipts, credit
cards, calculators. Inside some of the big notebooks are slots
into which you're supposed to put little notebooks.

There are gizmos they call portable offices, which are
zippered mini-cases with mini everything inside. Mini-tape
measure, mini-stapler, mini-scissors, mini-tape dispenser,
mini-paper clips, mini-rulers. The mini-case is designed to
be thrown inside your briefcase. Your briefcase is probably
full of slots and sections and compartments, too, all of which
are supposed to keep you on top of your life.

Unfortunately, the individuals who are best able to use
all these cases inside cases and slots inside compartments of
subsections inside sections of folders, are those who are extremely well-organized to begin with. People like me who
truly need to get their acts together would never remember
what part of which organizer we had put anything in.

But I'm definitely going to get organized. One of these
days.

Pockets

I have always operated on the assumption that the reason they put pockets in men's clothes is so you can put stuff in there. The average pair of pants has four pockets. One on each side and two hip pockets. The average jacket has five pockets. One on each side, a breast pocket, and two inside pockets. If you wear an overcoat or a raincoat, that gives you four more pockets to deal with, for a grand total of thirteen. Ordinarily, I carry stuff in all thirteen pockets.

Right now, for example, I have my wallet with the credit cards and the pictures of the family and the press card in my right pants pocket. On top of the wallet are the keys. The house keys, the car keys, the office keys, and two or three others that I'm not so sure about, but am afraid to throw away because they probably unlock something that I'm going to need to unlock one of these days.

In the *left* pants pocket are twenty-five dollars' worth of bills, seventy-seven cents in change, a pocket calculator, and a Swiss Army knife. The Swiss Army knife has fourteen different tools in it, including a pair of scissors, a corkscrew, a can opener, and a magnifying glass, all objects I could probably do without most days. The problem with the Swiss Army knife is that it tends to bore a hole in the bottom of any pocket you put it in. This cuts down on the number of pockets available, and therefore increases the load on the remaining pockets.

In my left hip pocket is a stopwatch on a chain, and in the right hip pocket are two subway tokens and a pocket comb. This is an on-the-spot inventory. I also know that in my suit jacket pocket are a handkerchief, a pair of glasses, a bow tie, and a ballpoint pen. In the inside jacket pockets are a checkbook, a pocket calendar, and a piece of paper with a telephone number written on it. No name, just a number. I'm afraid to throw it away because I'm afraid I might need it, but I haven't the foggiest idea whose number it is.

I wish I could say that there is some kind of system to all of this, and that I always know exactly which pockets to look in for the checkbook, the wallet, the press card, or whatever. What usually happens is that I pat the clothing from the outside to *feel* where things are. This works all right with the wallet, the Swiss Army knife, and the key ring. It is not too good with the checkbook and the telephone number.

Last night I parked the car in a parking lot and couldn't remember what I did with the parking-lot ticket. Patting doesn't help you find parking-lot tickets, either. There is something unsettling about digging through thirteen pockets, pulling out wallets and stopwatches and Swiss Army knives, looking for the only little document that is going to get you your car back. I found it in the pocket with the eyeglasses, by the way.

In *Gentleman's Quarterly*, you never see men who look as if they have a lot of stuff in their pockets. Loaded pockets tend to spoil the lines of the clothes, or so the fashion experts say. Which probably explains why I've never been asked to *pose* for *GQ*.

I'm not really shaped like this. It's just the stuff in my pockets. Not much to look at, but if you happen to need a corkscrew, I'm your man.

The Key to Success

When I tried to get into my office this morning, I couldn't do it because I couldn't find my keys. They weren't in the usual pants pocket or the other pants pockets. Retracing my steps I discovered, to my increasing dismay, that I hadn't left them in the newsroom or the cafeteria or the men's room, or in my raincoat.

Surely, I hadn't left the keys in the car, had I? I tried to remember parking, shifting into Park, turning off the lights and the radio, and taking the keys out of the ignition, before getting out of the car. It was then that the sneaking suspicion hit me. I could remember everything except taking the keys out of the ignition.

A trip out to the street confirmed my sneaking suspicion. The car was locked, and clearly visible through the windows were the keys. They were hanging there, sticking their tongue out at me from the ignition, right where I had left them. On the ring, along with the car keys, were the front-door key, the back-door key, the office key, and several other assorted unidentified keys. I don't know what these other keys are for, exactly, but, as I've explained, I'm afraid to throw any of them out.

Everybody knows what you do when you've locked your keys in the car. You get a wire coat hanger. Now there is no shortage of wire coat hangers in this world, indeed the world may well be swallowed alive one day by wire coat hangers. But wire coat hangers are like policemen. You can never find a wire coat hanger when you need one. You find wooden ones and plastic ones, and ones that are half plastic and half wood. Finally, I found what I needed.

Which brought me to the next problem. Once you obtain the wire coat hanger, how are you supposed to open the car door with it? My car doors don't have the little buttons that lock and unlock the door. You have to unwind the hanger and stick the wire between the glass and the window frame, and fish around with your end of the wire trying to hook the door handle on the inside. This is a fiendishly difficult operation, very much like brain surgery, I would imagine, and one which takes a long, long time to accomplish.

While you are standing there in the street, working with intense concentration through the window with the coat hanger wire, passersby give you the strangest looks. Some of them, I'm sure, had me figured for a car thief. Others had lots of advice and stopped to give me a little commentary on how such things can be avoided, and failing that, how to succeed with a wire coat hanger. It made me wonder if professional car thieves get all that unsolicited advice when they're breaking into people's cars.

Finally a stranger came along, a young guy carrying a little bag. "Let me give you a hand," he said. He drew a long thin flat rod from the bag, glanced furtively up and down the street, inserted the long thin flat rod into the door frame, flicked his wrist, and like magic, the door lock opened.

"That's terrific," I said. "Thank you very much." "Think nothing of it," said my Good Samaritan. "See you on the radio." And off he sauntered around the corner. Golly, that sure was nice of that fellow, I thought to myself. I wonder what he does for a living. On second thought, don't ask.

The Cord Conspiracy

The other night, I was looking for some cord to wrap a package with. I knew there had to be some cord around the house because I distinctly remembered running out to buy some a few months ago, the last time we needed some cord.

I remembered thinking at the time that the smallest unit of cord available, a whole spool, was enough to tie up a Boeing 747. Much more than I needed, but at least there would be plenty left over for the next time.

Now it was next time, and there was no cord. The first place I looked was in the bottom drawer of the kitchen cabinet, next to the sink. It seemed to me I had seen the cord in there dozens of times while searching fruitlessly for the hammer. This time, the hammer was in there but the cord wasn't. Had it been the hammer I was looking for, you know what would have been in there, don't you?

I asked Jean, my wife, if she had seen the cord, and she said no, but suggested looking in the bottom drawer of the kitchen cabinet. Not the one next to the sink but the one next to the stove. There, I found several curtain rod fixtures, some nails, the top part of the broken waffle iron, a pair of pliers, and a container of glue. It was the sort of drawer cord ought to be in, but there was no cord.

Nor was there any in the middle drawer of the chest in the pantry or on the shelf in the closet in the back room, or down in the basement in the box under the wood table, although there had been reported sightings in all these places by one member of the family or another.

After looking in every conceivable place and coming up empty-handed, I had to go buy some cord. I began to suspect, however, that a clever ring of cord-and-hammer thieves must be operating in our part of the country.

Then, the awful truth dawned on me. They would deny it, of course, but I am convinced the manufacturers of cord and hammers design their products in such a way that they cloud men's minds. You may remember when you used it and how, but never what you did with it when you were through. You must run out and buy more and more and more hammers and more and more and more cord every time you need to nail something or tie something up.

Over the last ten years or so, I must have bought approximately seventy-five hammers and ten or twelve miles of cord. The man at the hardware store has no idea what I do for a living, but I'm sure he figures it is something that involves the use of hammers. Many, many hammers.

And the woman at the variety store where I buy the cord probably has been puzzled about what this strange character could possibly be doing with all that cord.

Neither has ever inquired about it directly, but if they ever happen to meet each other and discuss the buying habits of their customers, I'll bet anything I come up in the conversation. Little do they realize that I hardly *ever* have occasion to hammer anything or tie anything up.

Somewhere in this house there is a fabulous hammer-and-cord collection, and one of these days I'm going to find it. While searching for the pliers, no doubt.

Think back. When was the last time you needed some cord? You had to buy some, didn't you? And then, what did you do with it? Go look. I dare you.

The Art of Packing

There is an art to packing a suitcase. The seasoned traveler (such as I) learns how to fold and place everything just so. Socks here, shirts there. A place for everything and everything in its place. Most of my trips are only one or two days long, so one bag will usually do it. A carry-on hanging bag is a must, so there's no waiting for luggage at the airport after you arrive, and no possibility of your bags traveling to Buffalo while you're traveling to Kalamazoo.

But little business trips like that are not the true test of the artful packer. The true test is a family vacation. I'm not talking about a car trip, either. On a car trip, the automobile itself becomes a kind of suitcase. If you have forgotten to pack something and remember it at the last minute, you can just chuck it in the backseat or the trunk. You call that packing?

Watch me here as I demonstrate the fine art by putting 140 pounds of stuff into a bag designed to hold a maximum of 20 pounds. The bag itself is important. It must be of cloth or canvas with soft, expandable sides. The importance of this you will appreciate as we go along.

The first thing you do is decide which compartments will be reserved for what. My bag has one plastic-lined pocket for toothbrush, contact lens case, razor, shaving cream, etc. Anything that might be wet or might leak goes in there. By the way, if you're in the habit of putting an aerosol can of shaving cream in there without the cap on, you are asking for real trouble. I learned this the hard way one time in Evansville, Indiana. Have you ever seen a suitcase full of clothes in which every article has been saturated with menthol-scented Noxzema? I have, and it is not a pretty sight, believe me.

The second thing you do is take the clothes you particularly don't want to get wrinkled, carefully fold them, and place them neatly on the bottom of the bag. This would include slacks, jackets, neckties, and dress shirts.

On top of that you put the socks, the shorts, and the sweaters. Some people put their backpile of magazines between the shirts and the socks. I do not recommend this. When I did that in 1984, a picture on a magazine cover printed itself in full color on one of my shirts. This would not do. As an unbiased newsman, I could not very well walk around with a decal of Geraldine Ferraro on my shirt.

On top of the socks and shorts, you put several pairs of shoes. It is best to pack shoes with shoe trees inside. The combined weight of shoes and trees creates the illusion that you are carrying a bag of bricks. On top of the shoes you put the pajamas, the bathing suit, and the beach robe. This is a vacation, remember?

When finally you are ready to close the bag and zip it up, you discover the zipper will not zip because the bag is too full. So, you pull up on the sides of the bag, while pressing down hard on the contents thereof with your right foot. This compresses everything nicely and, in fact, makes enough daylight at the top to accommodate the things you have forgotten, which include: a hairbrush, a portable radio, the camera, the binoculars, two tennis rackets, a Frisbee, and a copy of *Lonesome Dove*. *Lonesome Dove* may be great reading, but it's tough packing.

You will have to struggle with the zipper again, but this time you hesitate to use the old foot trick for fear you will break something, put your foot through a camera lens, or a racket head. Still, you manage to get the thing closed and zipped somehow. And although the bag is grotesquely misshapen, with protrusions resembling shoes, tennis rackets, and *Lonesome Doves*, you can take pride in having once again successfully defied the laws of physics.

Cereal

———

In France, when I was over there recently, I bought a box
of cornflakes. This was an exceedingly un-French thing to
do. The French eat croissants for breakfast (or "little lunch,"
as they call it). They eat brioches or pain au chocolat. Sometimes they pour powdered chocolate and hot milk into a bowl
and dip pieces of baguette into it, or they pick up the bowl
by the ears and slurp it down without benefit of spoon or
cup. But the idea of "breakfast cereal" as we know it is
completely foreign to them. Foreigner that I was, however,
and perhaps homesick for a little touch of America, I bought
this box of cornflakes.

On the box I was fascinated to find serving and eating
instructions, which translate as follows:

1. Open the box.
2. Pour the cereal into a bowl.
3. Add milk (and sugar and fruit if you so desire).
4. Eat with a spoon.

We Americans might wonder how else one would go
about eating cornflakes. Were it not for the instructions,
might a French person attempt to consume the cornflakes
without first opening the box? Bite right into the box or
something? Having opened it, might he pour the contents

into a glass or onto a flat platter of some kind rather than into a bowl? Would he be likely to add salt and pepper, or some other spice or condiment? Might he attempt to eat the cornflakes with a fork? Or with his bare hands, maybe? You just never know. The cereal manufacturer (American) was taking no chances.

Expanding world markets are important for the cornflake business because here at home, not to sugarcoat it for you, the business has been suffering at the hands of oats. Oats and oat bran, in various forms including oat flakes, oat rings, oatmeal, etc., have become the "in" breakfast food. The cereal ads and boxes now read as if oats were the greatest thing since snake oil. The main gist of the copy seems to be that if you eat oats in the morning, you are less likely to drop dead of a heart attack in the afternoon, provided that you eat enough oats to choke a horse, combined with a program of diet, exercise, and clean living.

The Kellogg people, who made a fortune with corn-flakes, bran flakes, wheat, and Rice Krispies, are now re-acting to the oat boom by coming out with no fewer than three new oat cereals: one called Oat Bake, one called Heart-wise, and another called Common Sense. We could all do with a little common sense every day. Unfortunately, that kind of common sense doesn't come in a box.

But the corporate battles at Battle Creek, Michigan, Kellogg's headquarters, have apparently already brought down the company's president and chief operating officer. Oats have not been good for the blood pressure of certain Kellogg's executives, I can tell you that.

The Quaker Oats people must be tickled pink by the oat mania. But if I had been able to find a couple of their other products in France, I probably would have bought them instead of the cornflakes. I would have bought Puffed Wheat or Puffed Rice. When I was a kid these were the breakfast foods advertised on the radio as "The Cereals Shot From Guns." You can't get any more American than that.

The Potato Museum

I'm not sure what it means, but there has been a great proliferation of museums lately. In New York City nowadays, if you say you are going to the museum, that *could* mean that you are going to the Metropolitan, or the Museum of Modern Art, or the Whitney, or the Guggenheim, or the Frick, or the Museum of Natural History. Or it could mean that you're headed for the Museum of the City of New York, or the Brooklyn Museum, or the Museum of Broadcasting, or the Dog Museum. Yes, that's right. I said Dog Museum. There is now a museum devoted entirely to dogs. Statues of dogs, paintings of dogs, dog artifacts, and dog memorabilia. It could be argued, of course, that if you can justify a Broadcasting Museum, you can certainly justify a Dog Museum. Over the centuries, the dog has made at least as great a contribution to mankind as broadcasting. Even so, when I first heard about the Dog Museum, I thought, "Only in New York."

But I just now heard about a museum in Washington, D.C., that I hadn't realized was there. I knew about the National Gallery of Art. I knew about the Smithsonian, the Museum of Air and Space, the Corcoran. But I did not know about the *Potato Museum*. Not far from the Library of Congress, it seems, there is a special museum devoted entirely to the potato. The Potato Museum is now part of the Washington cultural scene, believe it or not. Tom and Meredith Hughes have done for the spud what the Dog Museum people have done for the dog. The Hugheses tell me that the potato industry does not sponsor or underwrite the Potato Museum. It grew out of their own fascination with potatoes. Some years ago, they were living in Brussels, and it was there that they began to collect potatiana. Offhand, I would have thought that Brussels sprouts would have caught their fancy, but it seems that even in Brussels there are more potato fanciers than there are Brussels sprouts fanciers. The Belgians and French do not refer to French fried potatoes as French fried potatoes. They call them "fried apples." I swear they do. The potato is called "pomme de terre," or "apple of the earth," in French. Fried potatoes are called simply, "pommes frites." Don't ask me what they call fried apples. They probably call them fried potatoes. At any rate, the Hugheses also publish a monthly potato magazine, called *Peelings*. The Hugheses' collection on display at their Potato Museum includes a poster of Marilyn Monroe wearing a potato sack, and an entire section devoted to the military potato.

Now it happens that I have had some experience with the military potato. This was in the days before there were such things as potato peeling machines. KP, back then, meant spending long hours separating potatoes from their skins. At that time, I'm sure there was nobody at Fort Dix who would have envisioned a Potato Museum in the nation's capital. Little did we realize that some day people would come and study pictures of GIs peeling potatoes.

At the Potato Museum there is also potato sheet music ("You say patehto and I say potahto"), potato records ("The Mashed Potato" by Chubby Checker), along with assorted potato machinery: peelers, mashers, slicers, etc.

Next time I visit Washington, I mean to pay a visit to the Potato Museum. I've never been to a potato museum before, so I don't know exactly how you're supposed to act there. But I suppose it's like any other museum. You're supposed to stand and look respectfully at each exhibit, perhaps stand back from it a bit and try to grasp the subtleties of it. If there's an abstract representation of some mashed potatoes, you don't ask what it's supposed to be. (Maybe it's *not* abstract, come to think of it. Maybe it's supposed to be like the mashed potatoes in *Close Encounters of the Third Kind* where the guy molds his mashed potatoes into a mountain.)

I suspect that my favorite exhibit is going to be the poster of Marilyn Monroe in the potato sack. I don't know much about potatoes, but I know what I like.

The Great Shirt Button Controversy

American men have been complaining a lot about the buttons on their shirts. For some reason, according to recently published reports, the buttons seem to be falling off, breaking, chipping, cracking, and otherwise disintegrating while the shirts are still quite new. Sometimes the button is completely gone. Other times there is a fraction of a button left. A shirt with one-half or one-quarter of a button is not going to stay buttoned for very long.

Why this is happening is a matter of much controversy. The big American shirtmakers say the buttons are not self-destructing. There is nothing the matter with the buttons, they say. It is all the fault of the commercial laundries. The automated equipment that's now used in many laundries may clean, press, and fold shirts neatly and efficiently from the laundry's point of view, but the shirtmakers contend that some of this machinery is death on buttons.

The laundry industry is not about to take that explanation lying down. Maybe once upon a time shirts would come back from the laundry minus buttons, they say. But now very often the better laundries check each shirt before they do anything else, to see if buttons are missing and replace any that are. So men's shirts are likely to come back from the laundry with more buttons than when they went in. The reason buttons are crumbling is not that laundry equipment is no good, they say. It's because the buttons are no good. The laundry people blame the companies that make the shirts. To cut costs and thereby increase profits, the major American shirtmakers have been buying cheap, inferior buttons. If that were true it certainly wouldn't surprise anyone, since it seems any company that makes anything these days is constantly on the lookout for cheaper methods and materials to use. But the shirtmakers deny they're playing any cost-cutting games with buttons.

If anything, they say, in response to the damage the laundries have been inflicting on buttons, the shirt manufacturers are working with engineers and the button industry, trying to come up with a better button compound, one that can withstand all the button punishment the nasty old laundries have been dishing out. Perhaps some space-age substance designed to withstand meteor showers and the heat of re-entry might do the trick.

I am not about to say who is right and who is wrong in this button controversy. But I do have a suggestion that might be helpful. I think the shirt companies should staff their button departments with people from the pin department. The most conscientious workers in the world must be the shirt company employees who fold new shirts in the first place, and pin them up. They pin the front to the back, then they pin the bottom to the top, then they pin the sleeves to the shoulders, the shirttail to the collar, and the elbows to the cuffs. They think of places to put pins that the customer would never dream of looking. When you put a shirt on for the first time you stand an excellent chance of stabbing yourself in the back.

Put these pin people in charge of the buttons, and those buttons aren't going anywhere!

Improvements

I recently saw an ad for a commuter airline about a new, "improved" baggage service. The improvement is that instead of the airline carrying your bags out to the plane, *you* get to carry the bags out to the plane yourself. This is typical of what passes for improvement these days.

When they say any service has been "improved," what they usually mean now is that they've figured a way for you to do it so that they don't have to do it.

In a bank, you used to hand your checks and deposit or withdrawal slips to one of the tellers, and he or she would put the slips in different places and push different buttons and then hand you the cash or deposit receipt. Now they have improved banking service so much that nobody does anything for you. Instead of waiting on line for a teller, you wait on line for a machine. Then *you* push all the buttons yourself. Then if there's any mistake, you have only yourself to blame. This may not be better for you, but it's better for the bank.

It started with the supermarkets. I can remember when you'd go to the grocery store and tell the grocer what you wanted and he'd find it, take it down from the shelves, and put it in a paper bag for you. Now things have improved a lot. You find it. You lift it into the shopping cart and later onto the checkout counter. About half the time you bag it yourself, and carry it out to the car yourself. I don't mind doing all this, you understand, but I fail to see in what way it is better.

To make a long-distance phone call, all you used to have to do was tell the operator what city and phone number you wanted. She'd get it for you. Sometimes you'd hear her talking operator-talk to some other operator, with codes and all that. Now you are your own operator and do all the work yourself. This may not seem like such a good idea to you, but it seems like a wonderful idea to the phone companies.

There used to be an elevator man in our building. His name was Bill. Bill knew what floor I got off on. I never had to tell him. He ran the elevator, opened and closed the door, and we would exchange a word or two about the weather. Several years ago, Bill was replaced by a panel of buttons. The doors open and close by themselves. Sometimes they close while somebody is standing right in the doorway. The doors don't care. They are the new, improved doors that go with the new, improved elevator.

The fellow at the gas station used to pump the gas into your car. He would also volunteer to check your oil and would always wipe your windshield. Now, under the new, improved kind of filling station, unless you want to pay more for it, *you* pump the gas. You check the oil. If you're lucky, they'll lend you a rag to wipe the dipstick. And if you expect to see through the windshield, you had better wipe it yourself. They will lend you another rag. Or more likely the same rag.

I am not sure we can stand very many more of these improvements. It is clear now that when companies tell you they're doing things *better* now, they don't mean better for you. They mean better for them.

The Mother of Necessity

They used to say that necessity was the mother of invention. Perhaps that was true in the old days, but it isn't true any more.

In the old days you needed something and somebody came up with an invention to fill the need. Now that we are in the new days, invention has become the mother of necessity. The invention comes first and the need comes later. Somebody invents something, and the hard part is coming up with some use to which the invention can be put. Once that has been taken care of, the invention quickly becomes so indispensable that we couldn't get rid of it even if we wanted to.

Nuclear bombs are a good example. The world really didn't need nuclear bombs. Mankind had managed to get along all right without nuclear bombs for a long, long time. But as soon as the atomic bomb was invented, it was used. And as soon as it was used, it became obvious that such weapons were dreadful in the extreme. And of course, as soon as we realized how dreadful nuclear bombs were, they became totally indispensable. World leaders have been trying to think of some way not to have nuclear bombs ever since, but have failed.

We didn't used to need computers in the old days. We muddled along somehow. People wrote books, got cash out of the bank, bought and sold theater and bus tickets, and talked on the telephone without using computers because there weren't any computers. However, as soon as computers came along, it became completely impossible to do any of these things *without* a computer. The more we began to suspect that our lives were being run by, and ruined by, computers, the more it became obvious that society could not function without them.

The cycle is always the same. First we don't need and don't have something. Then somebody invents it. This is how I know what is going to happen next.

Right now there is no way to get from the East Coast to the West Coast in twelve minutes. This is no problem, because very rarely does it come up that anybody *needs* to get from one coast to the other in twelve minutes. However, on the drawing boards of various aerospace companies, and in the budget planning of the Pentagon, is a combination jet airplane and rocket ship that will be able to do exactly what nobody needs to be able to do right now. It will be able to fly from New York to Los Angeles, say, in exactly twelve minutes. It will travel at thirty times the speed of sound. The experts say that a prototype could be built within the next five or ten years.

The "aerospace plane," as it's called, will cost billions of dollars to develop, and billions more to produce. Some will argue that the money should not be spent since we do not *need* to get from coast to coast in twelve minutes. This, as I have demonstrated, has absolutely nothing to do with it. We won't have it because we need it. We'll need it because we have it.

VI

SEASONS

A Long, Hot Winter

For most of the time that man has inhabited this planet, he has sweltered in the summertime and shivered in the wintertime.

This figures, since in most places it is colder in winter than it is in summer. But in recent times our species has taken to sweltering in the wintertime and shivering in the summertime.

I'm talking about indoors. We now heat our buildings in the winter to a sizzling temperature that we would regard as unacceptably hot in the summertime. And in the summertime we air-condition our buildings to a point we would regard as cruel and unusual punishment in the wintertime.

What has made possible this remarkable indoor reversal of the seasons are two of man's cleverest inventions: overheating and overcooling. Overheating was invented by the cave man shortly after the discovery of fire.

Overcooling was first used in 1952 at the Fontainebleu Hotel in Miami Beach, Florida.

To this day you will see women wearing furs in Miami in July and August. These women know what they are doing. In the hotel lobbies and restaurants of Miami, you need a fur to keep warm during the frigid indoor summer season. These furs, and other clothing designed to protect against the cold, are of no use up north during the stifling hot indoor winter season.

Whether you are north or south, and whether it is summertime or wintertime, you are making a mistake if you dress for the outdoor weather. Unless you plan to spend the whole day outdoors, that is. Certain breeds of dogs, cats, and other domestic animals that are kept indoors have adapted to man's ways. They grow long, warm coats to cope with the coldness of the summertime, and they shed that unneeded extra layer as the warmer wintertime approaches.

Overheating and overcooling have caught on to the point where if it is ninety degrees inside a department store, the customers are walking around sweating in their boots and overcoats. On the other hand, if it is forty degrees, that means it's air-conditioning season and the customers in their summer frocks are about to go into hypothermia.

Automobiles are "indoors" in this discussion. I know a driver of a car pool who turns the heater all the way up until his passengers are at the point of suffocation. Then, when somebody complains, he turns the heater all the way off and opens a window. The temperature drops about sixty degrees in ten seconds. Then somebody else complains, and he rolls up the window and turns the heater on full again. He goes through a seasonal cycle fifteen or twenty times on one trip.

In the summertime the process is reversed, of course, with the air conditioner providing the chill and the window letting the hot air in on cue. The heater and the air conditioner have two settings: all the way on and all the way off. And the windows have two settings, too: all the way open and all the way shut.

Extremism in the defense of climate control is human nature, I guess.

The Curious Drought

At the office there are signs on all the elevators warning about the drought emergency. We are not supposed to waste water, to let faucets drip, or to let water run unnecessarily. We are to report any dripping faucets or water wasting we see. All this in compliance with the New York City Drought Emergency Rules.

I live in New Jersey, not far from the George Washington Bridge. In the morning, it takes me only fifteen minutes to drive to the office. There's no traffic at 4 A.M. Still, it's not exactly another climate zone. If it's raining here, it's almost sure to be raining there. And it has been raining. This is the damndest drought I ever saw.

On the weekends, when I don't have to get up at 3 A.M., sometimes I sleep in until 6 o'clock or so. The other morning I did that, but even at 6 A.M., nobody else in the family seemed ready to get the day started. The only ones stirring besides myself were Max and Tony. Max is a sort of beagle. Tony is a Portuguese Water Dog puppy, seven months old. The three of us went outside into the morning.

It was not very warm for May. In fact, it was very chilly and damp for May. It had rained again overnight and everything was wet. The grass was wet. The newspapers in the driveway were wet. The old newspapers—the ones we had so carefully stacked and tied into bundles—were soaked

through. They were supposed to be picked up Tuesday. But
there they still were at curbside. They must weigh a ton by
now. Everything is waterlogged. Max seemed ready to go
back inside almost right away. Chilly, damp mornings and
soggy lawns do not especially appeal to him. Tony, however,
was having a ball. He scampered through the grass kicking
up a little wake behind him. Portuguese Water Dogs love
water. That's why they're called Water Dogs. Tony is hap-
piest when he hits a puddle. He loves to jump around in it
until his coat is thoroughly soaked. The only thing better
would be a lake, and the way things are going, it won't be
long now before there is a lake right there in the backyard.
When I bring him inside, he will drip all over the floor, I
know.

I walked across to the garden, my shoes squishing across
the lawn—*squish, squish, squish*. Some of the tulips that
had been standing tall were beaten down by the rain. The
earth around them was mud. The old song ran through my
mind:

> *Mud—mud—glorious mud—*
> *Nothing quite like it for chilling the blood*
> *So come with me fellow, down to the hollow*
> *And there we will wallow—in glorious mud.*

Back in the days of the oil crisis, there were some who
suspected that there wasn't really an oil shortage at all—that
the oil companies were manipulating the supply somehow
to jack up the price. This was not, in fact, the case. But
gasoline shortages give rise to paranoia.

And so do soggy droughts. Why would anybody want
to fake a water shortage? Don't look at me, pal, I don't have
the foggiest idea. Maybe there's a hole in the reservoir and
the water is leaking out. The official explanation is that there

was no run-off because there was no snow this past winter and all this rain has been falling above, below, and all around the reservoirs but not *on* them.

Anyway, going back inside to dry out, I noticed something on the front porch you don't generally associate with droughts—mildew.

Thinking About Vacation

There are two basic schools of thought when it comes to thinking about upcoming summer vacation. One school thinks you should think about it all the time, anticipating the great time you'll have, planning the logistics, savoring the enjoyable particulars in exquisite detail. The other school thinks you shouldn't be thinking that much about it. They feel guilty about thinking or talking about your prospective vacations. They think if your body isn't on vacation yet, your mind shouldn't be, either. Same thing goes for talking about summer vacation. Some people want to talk about it all the time. Others don't want to talk about it any more than they have to. The people who tend to think about it also love to discuss it at great length. The ones who don't want to think about it don't like to talk about it much, either. They enjoy vacation, they say, but only when it's vacation time.

Personally, I belong to the thinking-about-it-and-talking-about-it-all-the-time category. To me, the next best thing to sitting in the sun by the pool reading a good book and nursing a gin and tonic, is thinking and talking about sitting in the sun by the pool reading the good book and nursing the gin and tonic.

When a person in the thinking-and-talking-about-it school happens to be married to someone in the not-thinking-or-talking-about-it school, there is bound to be trouble. The conversations go something like this:

ME: You know what I'm really looking forward to this summer? It's sitting out next to the pool soaking up some sun, sipping on a gin and tonic, and reading a good book. That's what I'm really looking forward to.

SHE: That's nice.

Admittedly, there is nothing much about my revelation as to what I'm looking forward to that is terribly provocative or that provides much grist for the conversational mill. It's not as if I had announced my intention to take up skydiving or motorcycle racing. All it is is an opening, an invitation to further discussion of how it's going to be on the vacation. "That's nice" doesn't quite qualify as a satisfactory response. Something along the lines of, "Gee, I was hoping we could climb Mount Everest," would at least get a little dialogue going.

Our kids seem to take after me in this regard. Not that they are into sitting down very much. But there is some evidence that they belong to the thinking-about-summer-vacation-while-you're-still-in-school school. Even the day-dreaming-about-wind-surfing-while-you're-sitting-in-class class. A young person who is daydreaming about the fine points of wind surfing may have some difficulty concentrating on the fine points of history or math.

I know how they feel. When you get down to the last few weeks before vacation, it's hard, even for a diligent journalist such as myself, to think about the new leadership in Congress, the balance of payments, or the gross national product. You sit down to write, for example, and what pops into your mind to write about is thinking about and talking about summer vacation, and the sun and the pool and the book and the gin and tonic.

Are We There Yet?

This summer, for a variety of reasons, we Americans will be taking car trips and other family vacations in the good old USA. The open road beckons. Those of us who live in the northeast will head for the southwest, and vice versa. Disney World and Disneyland, Hollywood and Dollywood, the Grand Canyon and the Great Smokies are all expecting to do land-office business.

Every state has its attractions, and it's high time we loaded the kids in the car and took off to show them the glories that lie right in our own backyard. The trouble is that for many of us it's been a while since we took a family car trip, and we may have forgotten what it is like, exactly.

If taking a long car trip with the kids is something you haven't done, or haven't done lately, there are certain realities that should be pointed out.

1. Kids are not interested in scenery. Try as you will to point out the beauty of a lake or the majesty of a mountain range, your little ones will not give you the satisfaction of looking out the window.

2. What they will do most of the time is fight. They will fight about who gets to sit next to whom; they will fight about who gets to sit next to the window so they

cannot look out it. They will fight about who is taking up too much room. They will fight over books, magazines, toys, balls, pillows, and everything else they can think of. In the close confines of the family automobile, the decibel level will rise until you finally yell so loudly yourself that your voice can be heard above the din. The irony is that they will not get hoarse, but you will.

3. Twenty minutes after you have pulled out of the driveway, you will have to turn back because somebody forgot something. The entire vacation will be ruined unless you go back and get whatever it is. So you agree to do it, but with the understanding that this is absolutely, positively the last time on the trip that you will be doubling back to get anything. Anybody who leaves anything behind is out of luck, you will say. The next thing that gets left behind, by the way, will be your credit card at a restaurant. You will make an exception to the rule.

4. One hour into the car trip, you are certain to be asked how many more miles there are to go. Thereafter the question will be re-asked at least once every fifteen minutes. Starting at about the halfway point in the trip, the question will change to: "Are we almost there?" And then, in a whining tone: "Aren't we there yet?" At first you will try to give some sort of encouragement. "It won't be long now," or some such. But eventually, your patience will wear thin and you will hear yourself saying something like: "No, we're *not* almost there and I don't *know* how long it will be and shut up!!!"

5. It will be necessary to stop from time to time to eat, and to gas up. During these stops, despite all your urging, nobody will ever go to the bathroom. Only later, when you are driving out in the middle of nowhere, will you be notified of the urgent need for a bathroom stop.

The first few times, you try to oblige. Then, during the next meal-stop you announce that if everybody doesn't go to the bathroom while you're still at the restaurant, you will kill the next person who calls for an extra pit stop.

6. At some point during the trip you may wonder whether it was such a good idea taking this car trip after all. True, it may be highly educational and all that. But the *next* family car trip may be the one *your* kids take *their* kids on . . . a long, long time from now.

To Everything There Is a Season—But This Isn't It

You know what I hate about the fall fashions they're showing in the stores? What I hate is that they are showing fall and winter stuff, even though we are still in the dog days of summer. I don't like to buy winter stuff in the summer. I like to buy summer stuff in the summer and winter stuff in the winter. But in the winter when I'm ready to buy winter stuff, the only stuff they'll have out will be the stuff I wish they had now. This seems unnecessarily perverse, if you ask me.

I'm sure I'm not the only one who feels that way, but you'd never know it from what you find at the mall. Even if it's ninety-seven degrees in the shade, what any self-respecting men's retail establishment wants to tell you about at this time of year are the tweedy, woolly, fuzzy-wuzzy, back-to-school, cozy-warm sweaters and mufflers that I don't even want to *think* about in August, much less buy. Even to contemplate these articles in August will cause a severe case of heat rash.

Let me tell you the kind of guy I am. I am the kind of guy who only buys a raincoat on a day when it is raining. It's raining and I didn't bring a raincoat, so I go out and buy one. There is no way I am going to be motivated to go out and buy a raincoat on a beautiful, sunny day.

Nor am I likely, in the middle of January, to run out to the mall and buy myself a bathing suit or a pair of Bermuda shorts. But what are they selling at the mall in the middle of January? Why, "cruise wear," of course!

If you try to find an overcoat in the middle of winter, the clerks look at you funny, as if you just arrived from Mars. Or maybe they figure you've just been released from prison after serving a long sentence and need to acquire a whole new civilian wardrobe. Otherwise, why would you be doing something so bizarre as to shop for a winter coat in the winter?

I do not pretend to be a big marketing expert, but it seems just common sense to me that it should be easier to sell a man a sport shirt right now, when you can still fry an egg on the asphalt in the parking lot, than it would be to sell him a fur-lined parka with a hood. But the sport shirts are all picked over now, the department store people are living not in this season, but in the next, as usual. But you better buy the parka now. If you wait till the winter, you'll have to settle for a beach robe.

> *To everything there is a season*
> *At the clothing store,*
> *But when you need an item,*
> *They won't have it any more.*

The Robin and the Rose

Now that we're into September, it's time to start thinking about planting the flower bulbs again. Daffodils and narcissus won't bloom in the spring unless you plant them in the fall. So Georgia Crafton informs me. Georgia is my mother-in-law and the vice president in charge of gardening at our house. It's a good thing I do not hold that position since I know as much about flowers as Robert Benchley did.

Benchley once wrote of his limitations as a naturalist, confessing that when it came to matters ornithological (birds) or horticultural (flowers), he could identify only the robin and the rose.

Me too. As a city kid, I never had occasion to learn the right names for various flora and fauna. Now that I am a grown-up with a house and garden of my own, this gives me certain problems. Georgia Crafton spends all but the winter months living with us. This is very good for the garden, because when she arrives in the spring, the flowers seem to stand at attention to pipe her aboard. She calls the flowers by name, and sometimes by two or three names. Impatiens and sultanas, for example, turn out to be different names for the same thing. They come in various colors, too, which makes calling them the right thing even more difficult for me.

What she calls violets, I call the "little purple ones."

What she calls peonies, I call "the big round ones with the ants in them." Her hydrangeas are my "snowballs." The vine with the pretty orange flowers on it is *not* a flower. "That's a trumpet vine," she says, "and it's a terrible weed." So is honeysuckle, according to the vice president in charge of my garden. Near as I can figure out, anything that *wants* to grow out there is by definition a weed, and anything that you have to *coax* into staying alive is a flower. Some weeds are prettier than some flowers, if you ask me, but prettiness is not the test.

My job, when I am occasionally pressed into service, is to water the garden. This presents something of a communications problem, since I do not always fully understand the briefing that precedes execution of the mission. Certain plants like water on the top, but most would prefer to have their roots watered without getting their leaves wet, I'm told. How this is accomplished in nature, I do not quite understand since rain almost always comes downward from the sky. Then there are certain plants that like a lot of water and some that only like a little bit. This for the hostile lilies (I know that's not how you spell it, but that's what it sounds like to me), that for the begonias. Not knowing a begonia from a lazy Susan, I try to translate it all into terms I can understand: "The ones with the blue fuzz," "the big ones with the yellow stuff in the middle," or "the low-growing yellow and red ones next to the pretty purple ones."

"And not too much water on the *rose*bush," Georgia instructs me. "It'll mildew." And then, realizing that I may not have quite got the message entirely straight, she calls after me sweetly: "That's the bush with the red flowers and the thorns!"

Waking Up Is Hard to . . .

The first thing I always notice about September is not a chill in the air or the leaves. What I notice is how dark it is these mornings when I drive into the Broadcast Center in New York City. The daylight is getting squeezed on both ends now, the sun setting a little earlier, rising a little later. To tell you the truth, it makes me wish I could rise a little later myself.

People figure I must be used to getting up early in the morning after all these years, but it's not so. A morning radio colleague of mine says you never get used to it: You just get used to feeling rotten.

A long time ago, I discovered one of the greatest feelings in life. It is to wake up early on a dark, dreary morning dreading the thought of pulling yourself out of the sack, and then suddenly to realize it's Saturday and you can roll over and go back to sleep. When I was a kid, I found a variation on this principle and looking back on it now, I must admit it seems a little weird. If I had to wake up at seven in the morning, I would set the alarm clock for six, simply to enjoy the luxury of knowing I had another hour to sleep. How can you appreciate not having to get up yet if you are sound asleep, unconscious, and oblivious to your good fortune?

Pursuing the logic of this, I began to set the clock for 5 A.M., so that I could realize how lucky I was that I didn't have to get up for another two hours. I would reset the alarm for six so as not to miss the pleasure of knowing I had one hour to go and so on. For a while there, I took to setting the alarm for four.

All this was years ago. But just recently, I read the results of some sleep research done at San Jose State University by psychologist Robert Hicks. Hicks found that setting your alarm clock back a few hours can actually give you more pep during the day. His theory is that by interrupting your sleep toward the end of the night, you cut off the last dream cycle. He says it's that particular dream cycle that can leave you feeling lethargic. The bad part is that altered sleep patterns make people more aggressive. When I altered my bride's sleep pattern years ago, it made her more aggressive.

Nowadays, our five kids see to it that we do not get an extra minute's sleep—even if it is Saturday. As to alarm-clock experimentation, that's behind me now. But it seems to me that I've been hearing alarm clocks going off in my son's room at very strange hours.

Christmas Shopping

Kids never seem to have any trouble sitting down and writing a letter to Santa Claus. Making up their list of what they want for Christmas is easy for them because they always seem to know what they want. They have been watching the TV commercials and discussing the matter with the other kids, and by the time it's list time, they've got it all figured out. That sure is more than I can say.

I wish I knew what I want. It would sure make Christmas shopping a whole lot easier . . . for me and for everybody else on my list and on whose list I happen to appear. But, unfortunately, I don't know what I want. I don't know what I want to get for Christmas, and I don't know what I want to give, either. Not to other non-list-writing grown-ups, anyway. Not knowing what I want to get is OPP (Other People's Problem). But not knowing what to give them is MOP (My Own Problem). It's the same way every year.

I'm the sort of Christmas shopper you often see at this time of year wandering aimlessly and half dazed around the flag department. I'm looking for something, obviously. But I don't know what it is exactly. Exactly nothing! I don't have the foggiest idea what it is. I don't even know who it's for yet. It's for somebody on the list, true. But until I see the thing I want to buy, how can I know which person on the list will be the lucky gift-getter? See what I mean?

What you end up doing when you use this approach is buying something you think is sort of neat and waiting until afterwards to figure out who to give it to. (Or "to whom to give it," if you prefer the correct pronoun and not ending a sentence with a preposition.) It's only when you're putting the package under the tree on Christmas Eve that you begin to wonder whether Grandma really needs a large American flag.

This is known as the *bad* way of Christmas shopping. It might be all right if you had all the time in the world, and were trying to kill the clock. It might be okay if being pushed around in the crowds at a department store were your idea of a good time. But if you are like me, trying to squeeze the Christmas shopping in between other chores, and if rallying around the flag counter is not what you think of as quality time, the "let me see what I can find" method is not the best.

The clerks in department stores are practically no help at all. If you can get one to pay any attention to you, this soon becomes quite evident.

"I'd like to get something for Grandma," you say.

"What did you have in mind exactly?" the clerk wants to know.

"Something nice," you explain.

"Something nice, eh?" sneers the clerk.

It's obvious she had you figured for one of those shoppers looking for something rotten to give somebody.

"Isn't there something nice I could buy that doesn't come in sizes?" you respectfully inquire. This is how you wind up in the flag department.

The Claus Memo

Memorandum

FROM: Consulting Service
TO: S. Claus
RE: Operations

There has been a thorough departmental review of the Christmas operation. We have interviewed the entire staff, observed and analyzed the current methodologies and activities, and have concluded that some immediate reorganization and revision is necessary. Herewith is a summary of our recommendations.

1. LOCATION: The North Pole is not a suitable headquarters, in our opinion. It is not convenient to mass transportation, the climate is abominable, and there is absolutely nothing whatsoever to do on a Saturday night. We recommend a move to the Sunbelt, perhaps to the vicinity of Phoenix, Arizona.

2. SCHEDULING AND FREQUENCY: It is unnecessarily costly to insist that "Christmas comes but once a year," especially since it comes on the same day all over. The workload is thus unevenly distributed, with too heavy a concentration of effort leading up to the

25th of December. Our recommendation is that Christmas be rescheduled so that it always falls on a Monday, thereby creating another three-day weekend. In addition, we suggest that Christmas be celebrated at different times of the year, depending on when it is hottest and driest in a given locality. Christmas could still be observed in December in Puerto Rico, but in Maine and Michigan it should be moved to the middle of August. The objective should be to eliminate any possibility of a white Christmas anywhere. Card makers should stop thinking snow and holly and start thinking sand and cactus.

3. TRANSPORTATION: The sleigh has got to go. In Phoenix, a sleigh would not be needed anyway. This would result in a significant cost reduction. For one thing, you could dispense with the eight tiny reindeer. Distribution could be arranged through Federal Express, Purolator, or United Parcel.

4. PERSONNEL: We note that in your present location there at the North Pole, you have hired mostly elves to be employed in the workshop. In Phoenix, you will find a much larger work force to draw from, as well as modern, well-designed, air-conditioned space for them to work in.

5. DRESS CODE: The somewhat bizarre outfits currently worn by you and your staff, although perhaps all right for your present location, would be highly inappropriate for Phoenix. Our design people suggest that the ridiculous red suit with the red hat, matching fur collar and trim, and the black boots, be replaced by shorts and a sport shirt. And your old hat is definitely old hat. If you insist on one, a cowboy hat would be more like it.

6. IMAGE: In addition to new clothes, the entire Santa

"look" needs to be updated. With all due respect, Mr. Claus, your overweight, jolly image is definitely passé. There's now a new, streamlined Aunt Jemima, a new, youthful Betty Crocker, and a slimmed-down pair of Campbell Kids. Perhaps the time has come for you to step down and make room for a "lean, mean" Santa Claus.

None of this is personal, of course. We are just trying to be helpful. By the way, my kid says to tell you he wants a Rambo doll.

'Twas a Little Outdated

Get real. Nobody says " 'twas" any more. And everybody calls December 24th Christmas Eve now, not "the night before Christmas." Besides, a lot of today's people don't live in houses. We're in apartments, and although some of these apartments may have mice, they are just as likely to have rats. Or, if we're taking inventory of vermin, cockroaches. And nobody wears kerchiefs and caps to bed, and when you turn in for the night you don't "settle your brains" and you don't call it a "nap." So right off the bat you can tell that the old Clement Clarke Moore poem, "A Visit From St. Nicholas," is in serious need of updating.

I don't know exactly what dances in the heads of sleeping kids these days, but I am pretty sure it is not sugar plums. Furthermore, most modern windows have no shutters to tear open and no sashes to throw up.

And no chimney to come down with a bound. Even in those cases where there is a chimney, it is probably lined now and much too narrow for anybody to use to get inside. And even where there is a fireplace, it was probably sealed off to save fuel during the energy crisis.

As for St. Nicholas himself, the man sounds like a mess. Dressed all in fur, indeed. Hasn't he seen the ads, heard the commercials on the radio? If he is such a nice guy, how is it he's willing to dress all in fur from his head to his foot?

Doesn't he care about the poor animal who used to wear the fur? He should be ashamed of himself. About what you'd expect from a man so selfish he'd let himself be pulled around by eight tiny reindeer. At least you'd think he'd use full-sized reindeer, wouldn't you?

And look at those clothes! Is he neat and clean? In a pig's eye! All tarnished with ashes and soot and everything! What kind of example is that to set for the children of the world?

And smoking? Will you look at that smoke encircling his head like a wreath? Can you believe with all the government reports linking tobacco to heart disease and lung cancer, that this character is smoking a smelly old pipe?

Chubby and plump, my foot. He is fat, that's what he is! That broad face and little round belly might have been okay in Clement Moore's day, but it's not okay any more. And proof that he's overweight and out of shape is that disgusting little round belly that shakes when he laughs like a bowl full of jelly. And what's he laughing at, anyway? The living room furnishings? It's not very polite to laugh at somebody else's decor, is it?

So with all due respect, I would suggst revising the story, cutting it down a bit, and getting rid of some of the outdated concepts, such as charm and grammar. Something like this, maybe:

On Christmas eve, my old lady and me
Hit the sack 'cause there wasn't much good on TV.
The kids were asleep or pretending the same,
Dreaming no doubt of some video game.
When suddenly I heard the front doorbell ring.
Who is that, I wondered, and what does he bring?
To my wondering eyes, when I opened the door,
Stood a guy who looked straight from the Ralph Lauren store.
He was thin, he was neat, and extremely well-dressed

With a confident air, he was quite self-possessed.
I knew that it had to be this guy St. Nick,
For his style was so with it, so preppy and slick.
And I heard him exclaim, jumping in his Ferrari,
"Make your credit card payment or you will be sorry."

VII

SOME PEOPLE

Dumb Crooks

Cops and robbers used to be at least partly a game of wits. Seems to me America used to have a lot of smart criminals. Whatever became of them? Must have gone into some other line of work, I guess. Investment banking, most likely, or maybe defense contracting. Anyway, the crop of criminals we have now holding up our liquor stores and breaking into our houses is a pretty sorry lot, I'm afraid. To say that they are not terribly bright is understating the case. Almost every day on the newswires there is another story about some poor slob trying to pull off some kind of heist, only to bungle it all.

Last weekend in Malibu, California, somebody was making a videotape of a parakeet to study the bird's habits . . . and a burglar broke in while the tape was running. Watch the birdie! The shots of him were quite good. Enough to turn him into a jailbird.

In Sterling, Kentucky, an absentminded bank robber left his gun on a soda pop machine inside the Montgomery-Traders branch, then managed to lock himself out of the building. A newspaper photographer, Bobby Warner of the *Montgomery Times*, spotted the robber, hid behind a telephone pole and shouted: "Stop or I'll shoot!" The fellow spun around, Warner did shoot him, shot his picture, that is. Also got some nice shots of the arrest that soon followed. Robber

Robert Robinson is charged with first-degree armed robbery.

In Jackson, Tennessee, the other day, two men who apparently hadn't seen *Crocodile Dundee* walked into a convenience store and one of them pulled a knife on the only clerk in the store, Alesia Melton. "You call that a knife?" said Alesia. "This is a knife!" And with that she pulled out a foot-long machete. The men took one look at the machete and got out of there as fast as their legs could carry them.

Then there was Harold Schmidt of Waukesha, Wisconsin, who was arrested and charged with breaking into somebody's apartment a while back. All the Waukesha police knew was that somebody had broken in, stolen some necklaces and earrings, some tape cassettes, some vitamins from the medicine chest, and some frozen chicken patties from the refrigerator. Nobody would have realized that Harold was the alleged perpetrator except that he had this sudden urge, right then and there, to call up his grandmother in Florida. Something had reminded him of his grandmother. Maybe it was the jewelry. Maybe it was the frozen chicken patties. We don't know. But he picked up the phone and called her.

When the phone bill next came, the woman realized that she had made no phone call to Florida that night. And police contacted the grandmother who said yes, she remembered who had called her. It was her wonderful grandson, Harold. Harold now faces up to ten years in prison, for calling his grandmother of all things.

And last Sunday, when a Milwaukee woman walked into her house, she heard heavy breathing in the living room and found a man sleeping on her living room couch. The last thing she wanted to do was wake up Sleeping Beauty, but she tiptoed to the telephone, called the police, and over they came.

They roused Michael Brennan, searched him, and found on his person four necklaces, fifteen credit cards, four rings, and a tie tack, all belonging to the woman. Seems he'd had a few drinks earlier, and when passing through the living room on the way out spotted the sofa and couldn't resist lying down for just a minute.

Crime does not pay. I can believe it, especially with criminals like these.

Calamity Jane

Most of the time, thank God, the "news" is something that happens to somebody else. The floods and the explosions, windstorms and fires, earthquakes and mudslides happen all the time, but they occur in other people's backyards, not our own. We care about the disasters, natural and man-made, that comprise the day's news, because we sympathize with the people affected, even though we are not, with rare exception, personally affected ourselves.

However, if you play your cards just wrong, you can find yourself at the wrong place, at the wrong time, repeatedly. Cathie Kidrick is like that. She is not some roving news correspondent for TV. She is not a member of the fire department or a police SWAT team. Cathie does not belong to some military "quick response" unit, nor to the Red Cross. These people are supposed to go to disasters. Cathie is a thirty-three-year-old American housewife and mother of three small kids who just *happens* to be there when things happen.

For example, she was at home in Alameda, California, when the big Bay Area quake hit on October seventeenth. In a sense, she was lucky because she and the kids were unhurt, although the house was so badly damaged they can't live there any more. Cathie's husband, Jim, is a Navy fighter pilot. He was on duty on the *U.S.S. Enterprise* when the quake hit.

Cathie might have taken the kids and moved in temporarily with her relatives back in Charleston, South Carolina, were it not for the fact that her parents' house and the houses of her sister and brother were either wrecked or badly damaged in Hurricane Hugo.

Hurricanes are no stranger to Cathie. She was in Pensacola, Florida, when Hurricane Alice came roaring through in 1976. Jim was sent to the state of Washington for some flight training in 1980. There, in the shadow of Mount Saint Helens, she had a nasty scare when the volcano popped its top, spewing lava and ashes for hundreds of miles around.

Three months later, Cathie was in Corpus Christi, Texas, when Hurricane Allen hit. Two people were killed, damage was put at 53.1 million dollars.

It doesn't seem to matter what direction she goes in, or how far away. When Cathie and Jim went to Hawaii for a Thanksgiving vacation, Hurricane Iwa devastated the islands, causing $160 million worth of damage.

In 1983, Cathie was living near Coalinga, California, at the Lemoore Naval Air Station, where Jim was based. The quake that shook Coalinga was measured at 6.7 on the Richter scale. Jim was about to land his fighter plane when the ground started to shake and holes opened up in the runway. He had to land someplace else.

Now that another quake has rendered her home uninhabitable, and Cathie's South Carolina family isn't able to take her and the kids in because of Hurricane Hugo, Cathie's waiting for word to come that Jim is being transferred to Fallon, Nevada, where there's a Naval Air Station. It looks as if that will be their next duty station.

Just because Cathie Kidrick seems to have been a walking magnet for natural disasters in the past, it doesn't follow that she will continue to be so in the future. But if I were in Fallon, Nevada, I would worry.

Would You Believe
999 Points of Light?

In accepting the GOP nomination for President, and then later after he was elected, President Bush made reference to what he called "a thousand points of light." This was his way of saying that the U.S. government is not and should not be the only source of care and assistance for people in need. Mr. Bush wants to encourage Americans to help each other in every way possible through the private sector. As individuals, and through charitable organizations, we can express our concern for the less fortunate among us. That is the theory.

This is the reality. In Santa Cruz, California, forty-nine-year-old Sandra Loranger felt so sorry for the homeless and hungry people in her part of the country, that she wanted to help them in some very direct and personal way. She is the owner of an antique store, and her customers tend to be well-heeled people who can afford to indulge their taste for fine old furniture and the like. Sandra likes fine old things, too, but realized that there were many poor families who had no bed of any kind to sleep in, no roof over their heads, and not enough food to eat.

So she began making soup at home, and taking the soup to an open-air mall there in downtown Santa Cruz, and giving it away. When she saw how many people lined up to get the free soup and bread, she came back again and again. She was a "point of light," a private citizen seeing a need and trying in her own way to help. Some of the better-off folks shopping in the mall were offended by the sight of homeless people lined up to get a handout of soup and bread. Why should shoppers spending their hard-earned money have to look at such a thing? they reasoned. If do-gooders want to help the homeless, let them do it someplace else. Some of the merchants in the mall weren't thrilled about the soup lines, either. Before long, the local police were cracking down, demanding to see Sandra Loranger's permit from the county Health Department.

Since she had no such permit, Ms. Loranger was told she must cease and desist in this illegal and unauthorized giving away of soup and bread. You can burn the American flag without a permit in this country, but you can't feed homeless people without one. Sandra and some of her friends began wearing disguises when they brought the soup to the mall, realizing that if the cops spotted them, they would stop them from giving out the free soup and bread.

Four times Sandra was arrested. In June there was a jury trial. It lasted three days. She admitted that she'd been engaged in the unauthorized dispensing of free soup and bread to indigents for three months. Accordingly, she was found guilty. The judge offered her probation as an alternative to jail, but Sandra would have to sign a statement promising not to commit such crimes any more. She was not ready to say that, and was sentenced to forty-five days in jail. Because the jails are so overcrowded, it is expected that she'll only have to serve thirty days.

Since she does have some kitchen experience now, Ms. Loranger would not be at all surprised if they assign her kitchen detail. In that case, she may end up serving soup to some of her homeless friends who are doing time for violating the Santa Cruz ban on outdoor sleeping. In these days of criminal cooking, illicit feeding of the poor, and illegal outdoor sleeping, is it any wonder the jails are full?

I wonder if George Bush knows about this? I wonder what he'd say?

Ole Rockin' Chair's Got Me

There is something so soothing and soporific about a rocking chair that it can put you right to sleep. What it is, actually, is a cradle. When you want the baby to go to sleep, you rock the cradle. Rock-a-bye, baby. This is the first rock music most of us ever experience. Later, when the rocking gets harder and is combined with the rolling, sleeping is out of the question. But even much later in life, when our favorite tunes are the golden oldies, there's enough baby in all of us to remember that gentle rocking motion, and react accordingly when we encounter a rocking chair.

If the cradle is the symbol for babyhood ("The hand that rocks the cradle rules the world"), then the rocking chair is the symbol for retirement ("I'm not ready yet for a rocking chair!"). Olin Allen II of Wilmington, Delaware, is not quite ready for a rocking chair. He's sixty-four years old, and even by the most traditional of standards has a year to go before retirement. He's a radiologist who enjoys his work and may not retire for a good long time.

Still, subconsciously, he may be thinking about going the rocking chair route, since there is evidence that at least once recently he was trying one out. It happened one evening after a Chinese dinner. Allen had stopped at a Sears store, and was walking through the outdoor furniture section when he happened to spot a great-looking overstuffed swivel rocker. He went over to it and sat down, and started to rock. Nice and slow. Back and forth. Maybe it was the Chinese dinner. Maybe he was just a little tired. But after only a couple of nice and slows and a couple of back and forths . . . it was . . . Good night.

And there he slept. Slept right through the rest of the store's business hours, right through the sounds of closing up. And apparently none of the store employees noticed that the overstuffed swivel rocker in the outdoor furniture section had a man sleeping in it.

After a nice four-hour nap, Allen woke up, looked around, checked his watch and saw that it was 1:00 A.M. His movement was detected by an automatic sensor, which set off alarms. Security guards sprang into action and Wilmington City Police surrounded the building. Allen found a store phone and was standing there trying to figure out how to use it when somebody spotted him. He heard a voice saying: "We've got our robber!"

"You haven't got a robber," said Allen, torn between embarrassment and fear. He was afraid any time now somebody was going to start shooting at him. "You've got me! I just want to get the hell out of the store!"

Although store officials were a bit surprised that the clerical staff had all gone home for the night without noticing Sleeping Beauty over there in the outdoor furniture department, they accepted Allen's story right away. Police didn't even file a report.

If Olin Allen II comes back to Sears and buys that overstuffed swivel rocker, I wouldn't be a bit surprised. After all, he did take it for a nice test drive. Sort of like taking a new car out. But I hope if he ever does take a car for a test drive, he doesn't do the same thing.

David Wimp,
The Calculating Man

In Riverton, Wyoming, there lives a calculating man, a retired army cook named David Wimp. Since it's possible to retire after only twenty years in the armed services, Wimp is still a young man. He is forty-four years old. Some people might go out and get themselves another government job of some sort and retire from that after another twenty years. This is called double-dipping. You get not one but two retirement checks.

But this is not the sort of person David Wimp is. He is, as we say, a calculating man, and he calculated that since he put in his time in the army, including thirty months in Vietnam, and retired as a staff sergeant, that's enough for any one man. Maybe in some places an army staff sergeant's pay wouldn't be enough to live on very comfortably, but Wimp calculated that in his old home town, he could afford to live well enough on that money. So back he went to Riverton, Wyoming.

What do you do with yourself, though, when you're only forty-four and retired? Being in a position to do whatever he liked and being a calculating man, Wimp went out and bought himself a calculator and started to work. Although he is not a millionaire by any means and is unlikely to become one, David Wimp knows what a million is, better than almost anyone on earth. That is because he spends hours every day playing with his calculator.

One day he decided to see how long it would take him to get to one million just adding one, plus one, plus one, plus one, etc. Even if you enter a thousand ones an hour, it will take a thousand hours to get to a million. And Wimp was in no particular hurry. He would go over to the calculator whenever the spirit moved him, and peck away, adding up the ones. Then he really got into it and would spend more and more time at the machine.

It took him five years to get to the first one million, but by then the thing had become an obsession, so he just kept going. He now spends up to six hours a day at it, and sometimes even does it on the weekends, sort of absentmindedly while he watches TV. Wimp has taken to wearing a rubber thimble on his index finger, because that much banging away is hard on your finger.

It's also hard on the calculator. Wimp has worn out eight calculators in the last year and a half, has gone through at least 71,583 feet of paper. Recently he got the calculator up to three million. A man who has added ones to get to three million must derive a great feeling of satisfaction just looking at the number 3,000,000 come up on the machine. But once you've done that, it's time to quit, to go on to something new.

So Wimp started subtracting ones instead of adding them, counting down instead of up: $3,000,000 - 1 = 2,999,999$; $2,999,999 - 1 = 2,999,998$, etc., etc. Instead of spending less time at this, he now finds himself spending more. He stops to eat, of course, and take care of personal necessities. But just about every day he wakes up, rolls out of bed, turns on the old calculator, and starts subtracting his ones. A man's gotta do what a man's gotta do.

Wimp has been married and divorced three times. Not every woman is able to live with a man like David Wimp. But at least he knows what he is doing, which is more than you can say about a lot of people in this world.

No Good Deed Goes Unpunished

Good old Aunt Luella. Everybody in the family knew that even though she wasn't exactly super rich, Luella was there for you if you needed some assistance. Luella Wilson and her late husband had operated Wilson's Dude Ranch near Bennington, Vermont, for many years, and Luella had saved enough to be comfortable in her old age. At the age of eighty-six, she had her house and the ranch paid off and enough money in the bank to go south in the wintertime, and to help out her friends and relatives when she could. Luella had come through for the folks more than once in a pinch.

Now, though, at the age of ninety-one, it's a different story for her. A jury decided two years ago that Luella should pay $950,000 to a man she had never met in her life. This man had been hurt in an automobile accident in 1984. He was riding in the backseat of a car driven by Willard Stuart. Willard is Luella's brother's daughter's son. That makes him her grand-nephew. Three weeks before the accident, Willard had asked Luella for some money so he could buy a car, and she wrote him out a check. That was her terrible mistake.

Before the accident Willard had admittedly been drinking and smoking marijuana. He also hadn't bothered to get a driver's license. The injured passenger, Mark Vince, was an unemployed drifter who didn't know Willard all that well. In fact, they had only met in a bar a couple of hours before the accident. Vince himself was no stranger to trouble, having eighteen misdemeanor convictions on his record. That was beside the point, however. Vince's injuries were severe, and his lawyers decided there was no point in suing Willard, since he had no visible assets, or the car dealer who had sold Willard the car. No, they decided to sue Willard's old Aunt Luella, since there was some money there to go after, and a house and a dude ranch besides.

The jury never saw or heard from Luella Wilson. She had some medical problems and never was called to testify. So they never had a chance to feel sorry for her. But they saw this poor fellow wheeled into the courtroom, paralyzed from the waist down and with one leg amputated. They felt so sorry for him that they decided Aunt Luella was guilty of negligence and should pay Mark Vince everything she had, and then some. $950,000. Luella didn't have $950,000 or anything close to it. The insurance company to which she'd been paying premiums for sixty years decided she wasn't covered for any such thing as this.

So Vince's lawyers went after all Aunt Luella's assets, including her life savings, the house, and the dude ranch. They've all been attached. Luella can live in the house, but legally it's not hers any more.

A juror in the trial, Sally McVie, is quoted as saying: "I guess in our hearts we were afraid it could turn out like this, but we never saw her, and we didn't know if she had insurance or not."

Although a Vermont Supreme Court has upheld the verdict and the judgment against Luella Wilson, her lawyers are arguing that at the very least the car dealer should have been sued, too, since after all, he, and not Aunt Luella, sold Willard the ill-fated car.

Luella Wilson finds it extremely difficult to understand how this could possibly have happened to her. She always thought society would approve of being kind and generous to your friends and family. Now she knows what cynics mean when they say: "No good deed goes unpunished."

Lazy Lake

This is the story that asks the question: Does a lazy little village with one street, thirteen houses, and thirty-two people really need a full-blown airport study, a roadway study, a survey of traffic levels, and a policy for its "historic buildings"? In short, does it need a master Land Use Plan?

Actually, it doesn't matter whether the village of Lazy Lake, Florida, needs any of this. It's the law. The state's 1985 Growth Management Act requires that every city and town in Florida, regardless of size, has to have a master plan, whether the people there think it needs one or not. Lazy Lake made the tactical mistake of not applying for state money, a five-thousand-dollar grant the state was offering any town in Florida to hire a professional planning consultant to do the job. But the good people of Lazy Lake, law-abiding folks that they are, coughed up two thousand dollars of their own to hire their own planner, and they submitted his work to the South Florida Regional Planning Council.

Two grand or no two grand, the Regional Council didn't like what it saw. Possibly insulted by being offered a two-thousand-dollar plan instead of a five-thousand-dollar plan, the Council rejected Lazy Lake's submission because they said it was incomplete. It didn't address several burning issues the planners felt should be dealt with. "Where are you going to put your airport? What are you going to do about traffic problems, your shopping malls and such? How are you going to preserve your historic properties?"

"We don't have any historic properties," says the mayor of Lazy Lake, David Rushlow. "There is no lore of Lazy Lake. Washington never slept here."

Built in the 1940s on thirteen acres of land around an old rock pit, Lazy Lake does have a lake now, but the people insist they are no lazier than anybody else. It's just that they don't see why they should have to make plans for things they don't have any intention of doing. They see no need for a Lazy Lake Airport, for example. The Hollywood–Fort Lauderdale International Airport is only about ten miles away. That facility will take care of Lazy Lake's airport requirements just fine for the foreseeable future. But just saying that you don't need or want an airport isn't good enough for the official state planners. They want studies, surveys, projections. They won't accept the local government's own findings, by the way. They insist that the studying and projecting be done by a professional planner, a consultant who speaks the Planning language and knows the Planning buzz words.

There are no lazy employees of Lazy Lake. We can say that with certainty, because Lazy Lake doesn't have any employees at all. The streets, or rather the street—Lazy Lane is the only street in Lazy Lake—is patrolled by Boward County sheriff's deputies. It happens to be a dead end street, so the traffic flow is quite limited. You're either driving in or driving out, and that's it. No traffic lights, signals, or signs required except for the DEAD END STREET sign at the entrance.

A dentist, Sherwood Moore, serves as president of the Lazy Lake village council. He finds it's like pulling teeth dealing with this planning matter, and he tells me he suspects the whole Land Use Plan requirement is nothing more than a boondoggle and a full-employment program for bureaucrats.

It's easy to forget your manners,
When you have to deal with planners.
Planning is worthwhile but still,
There's such a thing as overkill.

That Lucky Old Son

With the passing of the Reagan years, it's as good a time as any to observe that history sometimes turns on seemingly trivial matters.

For example, if there had been jet airliners in 1937, or if a promising young Hollywood leading man by the name of Ross Alexander had not committed suicide, or if the Chicago Cubs had not done their spring training on Santa Catalina Island, Ronald Reagan would never have become President of the United States.

Let me explain. Dutch Reagan was then a sports announcer for radio station WHO in Des Moines. When it was decided that the Cubs would do their spring training that year on the California island Old Man Wrigley happened to own, young Reagan went with the team, since his major assignment for WHO was to announce the Cubs games. They went by train, of course, as teams did in those days. On the way home, Reagan stopped off in Los Angeles to catch the eastbound express train, and while he was there in L.A. he looked up a girl singer from Des Moines who used to work at WHO. Joy Hodges was her name, and she had moved to Hollywood and was then playing bit parts in the movies. Joy and Dutch had dinner at the club where she was appearing, The Biltmore Bowl. They talked about people and places in Des Moines, and about their respective careers, and the singer suggested to the sports announcer that while he was there he might want to chat with her agent, Bill Meiklejohn. Who knew at the time that this casual suggestion would have some impact on the history of the world?

Having nothing better to do the next day, Reagan called Meiklejohn, who took him to Warner Bros. to see the casting man, Max Arno. Arno asked the future President of the United States what seemed to Reagan a strange question: "Is that your real voice you are using?" Reagan assured him it was the only one he had, and Arno then explained that the Reagan voice was much like the Alexander voice. Actor Ross Alexander, who had been under contract to Warner Bros., had just committed suicide, so there was that rarest of things in Hollywood—an opening!

To make a long story short, Arno scheduled Reagan for a screen test the very next day. He and a contract actress did a scene from *The Philadelphia Story*. Arno asked Reagan to stick around for a couple of weeks since Mr. Warner was away and would be back then, and he'd be the one to make any decision. Reagan said he couldn't do that since he had to get back to his job in Des Moines.

Several days later, back at WHO, a telegram arrived from Hollywood offering Dutch a seven-year contract. Starting pay $200 per week, which seemed a fortune! Reagan couldn't believe his good luck and wired back that he accepted Warner's terms, and thus did sports announcer Dutch Reagan become movie actor Ronald Reagan.

If it weren't for that, he wouldn't have become a screen actor and therefore would not have become active in the Screen Actors' Guild. He would not have become a famous movie star and therefore would not have gone into politics and therefore would not have run for governor of California. It's reasonable to assume further that if he hadn't served as governor he would never have run for President.

And if Ronald Reagan hadn't become President? What then? Would national and international events have unfolded in quite the same way as they did over the last eight years? Who is to say?

History, like baseball, is a game of inches.

Samarkand in South Carolina

In the Samarkand legend, a servant encounters a woman in the marketplace at Baghdad and recognizes her as Death. The ominous figure looks into the face of the servant and makes what seems to him a threatening gesture. Trembling with fear, the servant runs home, borrows his master's horse, and rides all the way to Samarkand so that Death will not be able to find him. Later, the master sees Death and asks her why the threatening gesture. And Death says, "There was no threat. I was merely startled to see your servant in Baghdad, for I have an appointment with him tonight in Samarkand."

Every one of us has an appointment with Death, of course, but most of us do not know the particulars, the when, where, and how of it. Death knows, but we don't, unless we happen to be where Michael Anderson Godwin was for so long, waiting the anxious hours and days away on Death Row. Like the other inmates there, his mind was focused on the apparatus that was waiting for him, the infamous electric chair. He had been convicted of murder and the sentence was death by electrocution. When you know that to be your fate, it is difficult not to think about it.

But like most of the others on Death Row, Godwin kept hoping some way out could be found, some legal avenue that would let him escape the electric chair. And sure enough, it happened. There was a reprieve, a hearing, an appeal, and Godwin won a new trial. He was convicted this time, too, but now the sentence was not death but life. Life in prison. So there was a change, presumably, in Death's appointment book. But it was only in pencil.

Years passed. Having cheated Death, Godwin now lived at the Central Correctional Institution at Columbia, South Carolina. At first he was thought to be a troublemaker, but then he settled down and tried to make the most of his life, such as it was.

At night, the prisoners in their cells are permitted to watch television. But so that others will not be disturbed, the convicts must listen to the sound through earphones only. That was what Godwin was doing this past Sunday night. He was watching television, sitting naked on the steel commode in his cell, his back against the iron plunger, and with the earphones plugged into the TV set a few feet away. There must have been some problem with one of the earphones. He put the wire to his mouth while he fiddled with the earpiece. Perhaps he bit into the wire. That has not been established.

But later, when a guard called his name and Godwin did not reply, the guard unlocked the door, walked into the cell, and found Godwin's dead body still sitting there on the commode, the wire still in his mouth, his eyes wide open, and a grotesque expression of surprise on his frozen face. The steel commode had become an electric chair, and the high-voltage current had passed from the television set through the wire to the water in the steel bowl. It had passed also through Michael Anderson Godwin, killing him as surely as could any officially sanctioned lethal instrument of the state. Death had found him after all.

The coroner pronounced Godwin dead at the age of twenty-eight. Cause of death—accidental electrocution. "I was startled to see him in Baghdad," said Death, "for I had an appointment with him tonight in Samarkand."

The Magnificent Pain
in the Neck

They say "To get along, go along." They also say "Don't
make waves." And don't "ruffle any feathers," or "step on
anybody's toes." Someone who is trying not to "make any
waves," "ruffle any feathers," or "step on any toes," so he
can "go along" and therefore "get along," will make every
effort to "get with the program" and "go with the flow."
The person who fails to "get with the program" or to "go
with the flow" will surely be characterized as a "pain in the
neck."

Nobody wants to be a pain in the neck. Actually, these
days the pain is usually located somewhere to the south of
the neck. But that is neither here nor there. Most of us don't
want people to think that we are pains in the neck or any
other part of the anatomy, and will put up with pretty much
anything to avoid making trouble, and thus being regarded
as a troublemaker. The bigger the potential trouble, the more
out of our way most of us will go to avoid it. We will not tell
the boss what we really think of his new advertising cam-
paign. We will not complain to a restaurant about the quality
of food or service. We will not make a fuss about faulty
merchandise or goods of inferior quality. We want everybody
to love us, and if you're always moaning and groaning about
things, people aren't going to love you.

Andrey Sakharov didn't care about that sort of stuff. He
was never happy, always complaining. The mind that de-

veloped the Soviet H-Bomb could not bring himself to accept the illogicality and inhumanity of the communist regime. He kept criticizing, kept demonstrating, kept writing nasty things about the Soviet government and its sorry record on human rights. Sakharov was therefore regarded by the Kremlin as a great big pain in the neck. Leonid Brezhnev thought he was a pain in the neck. So did Andropov, so did Chernenko. For a while they put up with it, because he was who he was. Brilliant nuclear physicists are almost as hard to find in the Soviet Union as a good bar of soap.

They begged and pleaded with him to shut up, but he wouldn't shut up. They arrested friends and associates, and still he wouldn't get the message. Instead, he went to the showcase trials of the dissidents. Finally, they couldn't take it any more and exiled him to the city of Gorky. Even then he kept writing and talking about civil rights and ruffling feathers and stepping on toes, and being a first-class all-around pain in the neck.

It was Mikhail Gorbachev who finally realized that Sakharov couldn't be cowed, and let him move back to Moscow. Was Sakharov grateful? Did he reward his benefactor by not being a pain in the neck any more? Of course not. Gorbachev's *perestroika* and *glasnost* were all very well but not good enough. He wanted more effective *perestroika*. He wanted more extensive *glasnost*.

Even when he was in the newly formed Congress of Deputies as a member of the loyal opposition, Sakharov insisted on making waves and would not blindly go with the flow or get with Gorbachev's program.

Yet when he died, there was such an outpouring of affection and respect for Andrey Sakharov, that clearly people understood what Sakharov, the ruffler of feathers, the stepper on toes, had done for them. Thank God for the maker of waves. Thank God for the nagger, the nudger, the constant complainer. Thank God for the magnificent pain in the neck.

A Children's Song

"And *one* and two and three and four, and *one* and two and three and four and . . . *one* and two and three and four and . . ."

I'm sure there was nothing very musical or very moving about Robert Schumann's "Traumerei" from his "Scenes from Childhood." Not the way I used to play it when I was ten years old. It was a simple children's song, and a scene from my own childhood is me sitting there in Miss Dietsch's living room playing it with the metronone ticking out the slow cadence, and Miss Dietsch reminding me about fingers and elbows.

Matilda K. Dietsch, our piano teacher when my sister and I were growing up in Baltimore, used to tell us all the time to curve our hands and to make little hammers of our fingers, and to keep our elbows moving. Whether it sounded any good or not seemed to be beside the point. Miss Dietsch seemed always a happy piano teacher when she saw your fingers curved and your elbows bobbing up and down. She also used to tell us to listen to recordings by Vladimir Horowitz.

"Horowitz is the greatest pianist in the world," she used to say. And she'd put a Horowitz record, an old 78 rpm, on her own Victrola. Even through the cracks and the scratches of the low-fi audio of the day, you could hear that there was something very special about this Horowitz and his playing. I had visions of him sitting there at the concert grand piano, elbows bobbing and fingers curved and tripping away like little hammers.

Years later, when I finally got to hear Horowitz play live in a concert hall, it didn't sound like Horowitz to me. Where were the cracks and scratches? And it didn't look like Horowitz either. This was not the Vladimir Horowitz of Matilda K. Dietsch's fantasies. This Horowitz's elbows weren't bobbing up and down much. And his hands and fingers weren't curved at all. They were almost completely flat. The fingers were not nice even little hammers. They were long and slender, and they seemed to glide and snake over the keys with a life of their own.

Most every piano teacher in the world would tell you that was no way to do it, yet most every pianist in the world would tell you that Horowitz was the best. Number one. The sound that he produced was phenomenal. Who cared how he held his fingers if he could make music like that?

When the word came back that Horowitz died the other evening at the age of eighty-five, I went back to look at the videotape of his concert in Moscow in 1986. Here was this legendary figure who had not been home to Russia for sixty-one years. Soviet music lovers had been listening to his recordings for half a century. And now here was the man himself, frail and old, expected somehow to live up to the legend. It was too much to expect, really.

But he did it! He sat there with those flat fingers and non-bobbing elbows of his and played Beethoven, Scarlatti, Scriabin, and Chopin, all with such brilliant technique and virtuosity that it seemed nothing short of miraculous. The audience smiled and applauded, even cheered him with bravos at the end of each offering. But only during one selection did I see tears. Something in that one piece touched that Russian audience, moved them so visibly, that grown men and women were dabbing at their eyes with handkerchiefs. One burly-looking older Russian didn't even try to hide the tears. He just let them roll.

For there, in the land of his own childhood scenes, the great Horowitz was playing a simple children's song, "Traumerei" by Robert Schumann.